G000020206

THE FEARLESS PASSAGE

OF STEVEN KIM

Carl Herzig
with Steven Kim

WHITAKER
HOUSE

All Scripture quotations are taken from the *Holy Bible, New International Version*®, NIV®, © 1973, 1978, 1984 by the International Bible Society. Used by permission of Zondervan. All rights reserved.

THE FEARLESS PASSAGE OF STEVEN KIM:
The True Story of an American Businessman Imprisoned in China for Rescuing North Korean Refugees

318 Partners Mission
16 Godfrey Lane
Huntington, NY 11743
E-mail: 318partners@gmail.com
Web site: www.318partnersofnk.org

ISBN: 978-1-60374-729-5
eBook ISBN: 978-1-60374-730-1
Printed in the United States of America
© 2013 by Carl Herzig

Whitaker House
1030 Hunt Valley Circle
New Kensington, PA 15068
www.whitakerhouse.com

Library of Congress Cataloging-in-Publication Data (Pending)

No part of this book may be reproduced or transmitted in any form or by any means, electronic or mechanical—including photocopying, recording, or by any information storage and retrieval system—without permission in writing from the publisher. Please direct your inquiries to permissionseditor@whitakerhouse.com.

1 2 3 4 5 6 7 8 9 10 ⓤ 19 18 17 16 15 14 13

CONTENTS

PROLOGUE

Shackled upright to a wooden bench, the American peered through the scratched, grimy window as the train rumbled across the countryside. Farm after farm rushed by—countless villages whose names he'd never know. The sky was just getting light; it was not yet dawn. They were headed north.

He coughed weakly; the old carriage was thick with cigarette smoke and a sour human stench. They had just pulled out from a station, and a crowd of passengers speaking a dissonant hash of Chinese dialects pushed through the aisle to get to the next car. As they passed, they glared down with contempt at him and the nine other prisoners—three men and six women—all of them North Korean refugees headed to a *laogai*—a gulag, or labor camp—deep in the heart of mainland China.

They had been on the train one day and two nights, after being arrested in Chang'an and held for a night of screamed threats and insults in a concrete cell beneath the Guangdong Province Coastal Military Headquarters in Guangzhou. One of the men, an engineer in his mid-fifties, had been having trouble breathing. He'd gasped and wheezed, his florid complexion turning redder, then pale, then a bluish grey. They had been afraid he was having a heart attack, and hadn't known if he would last the night. When finally he had collapsed and lost consciousness, hardly breathing, they had called for the guards, who'd entered the cell and dragged him away. They hadn't seen him again.

The American's head throbbed, his back and limbs ached, and his throat burned from thirst. His lips were cracked and crusted with dried blood. None of the prisoners had had anything to eat or drink or even been allowed to use the toilet since boarding the train.

As the daylight increased, hunger turned into weakness. The American could tolerate that, but it was all he could manage to keep from emptying his bowels and bladder where he sat. Each point of pain competed with another. His ankles were red and swollen, manacled and joined together by a one-foot link. When during the long second night he had tried to get up and relieve the pressure, a guard had shoved him back down and locked his chains to the bench.

He rubbed at his wrists, chafed from the iron cuffs, but when he tried to lift and stretch his arms, a guard cracked a matte black baton against his knees and warned him in rough Mandarin, "Bie dong." *Be still.*

"How long?" he rasped.

"Bi zui," the guard told him. *Shut up.*

His mind roiled with stories he'd heard from the rare survivors of Chinese work camps—tales of rape, murder, forced starvation, torture. Young girls and boys rented or sold as sex slaves. Prisoners executed so their organs could be "harvested" and auctioned off to the highest bidder. At first, he hadn't believed the stories; however, as account after account had leaked out from one *laogai* after another, they had gotten harder to deny.

He strained to twist around for a glimpse of his fellow prisoners down the aisle. He could turn his head almost enough to see them, but they were too far away, and his torso was chained and bolted tightly to the bench. The others sat in pairs; only he was kept separate and alone.

The train stopped at one station after another—he had lost count long ago—and a new crowd pushed through after each stop, some settling down at the other end of the car. National Day, on the first of October, was only a few days away, and the whole train was packed.

The air around the prisoners became closer, stifling. He had lost all sense of touch in his hands and feet, but pain seared through his arms and legs, tore through his back, and cramped his stomach. He nodded in and out of consciousness, rocked by the jostling rhythm of the train. Now and again he fell into a fitful sleep, but he was jerked up every few minutes by the sharp burning of the metal cuffs and shackles cutting into his skin.

Hours later—it was now broad daylight—the guards came down the aisle and allowed the other prisoners, still chained to their partners, to use the toilet, located in a tiny restroom at the end of the carriage. They groaned getting up and then fell again and again as they stumbled down the aisle, supporting each other when they couldn't stand. One of the older women was fading; her eyes were dull and listless as her partner lifted her up and carried her along. The guards screamed and pushed at them to keep moving. The American knew some Chinese but doubted that the others—all North Koreans—could understand. Still, he was certain they'd gotten the message.

When the other prisoners were brought back, seated across from him now, the guards handed each one a few dry crackers and a cup of tepid, watery broth. He could see them concentrating so as not to spill, their hands trembling as they struggled to bring the cups to their dry lips.

Finally, the guards unlocked his chains from the bench and hoisted him up. His knees buckled; he felt sure his ankles would break. One guard on each side grabbed hold under his shoulders, dragged him down the aisle, and tossed him through the open restroom door onto the toilet, then stood there laughing as he struggled to loosen his pants in time.

When he was done, the guards hoisted him out, giving him no chance to wipe himself. He pulled up his pants and fastened them on the way back down the aisle. From the other end of the car, passengers craned their necks and stared with disgust.

The guards dropped him back on a bench across from the others, locked his shackles in place, and gave him two crackers and a cup of the dirty broth. Wetting his parched throat with the liquid, he let small pieces of the crackers dissolve in his mouth. Soon his head cleared just a bit. His hands and feet were on fire; his body screamed as feeling returned to his limbs.

As he sipped, wanting the broth, as repellent as it was, to last as long as possible, his nostrils flared at a new smell—pungent, garlicky, familiar—cutting through his own stink. He closed his eyes and inhaled deeply. "Kimchee," he mouthed—his favorite, a staple from his Korean upbringing and home. He exchanged sad glances with another of the prisoners—a young girl, no more than a teen, who had been arrested along with her mother. A group of passengers moved down the carriage, carrying bowls of rice and the salty, pickled cabbage back to their seats.

He thought of Helen, his wife. Her kimchee was the best. Tears welled in his eyes. He pictured Helen and their three children—Eric, Lisa, and Charles—safe in their big house in Huntington, on Long Island in New York. It was late Saturday night there, he figured. In the morning, they would go to church, and, after services, holding each other by the hand, they'd talk with their pastor, with friends, and with neighbors and other members of the congregation, accepting their love and support.

By now, Helen would know he'd disappeared. And she would worry. But none of them could ever imagine his actual position—what had happened in the last few days—and where he sat now, hungry, dirty, and smelling of his own excrement, shackled to a bench with nine other prisoners on a train hurtling deeper and deeper into a hellish oblivion at the heart of the mainland.

After he'd been arrested, he had tried to phone his office manager from the station house, hoping she would call Helen and tell her that he was in custody. Helen would have known what to do. But the guards hadn't granted him access to a phone, and then, almost before he'd known it, in the middle of the night, they had snatched him and the others from their joint cell, bound them in chains, and hurried them off to the waiting train.

They were a long way from home, he thought—the North Koreans but especially himself—and none of them knew when, or if, they would see their families again.

He looked up, roused from his despondent reverie. Across the aisle, two pairs of prisoners huddled together, all whispering at once, as if in unison. The guards were down toward the end of the car, eating with the other passengers.

He leaned forward, arching toward the group, straining to hear what they were saying. Through the smoke and the smells and the exhaustion they all shared, he could just barely make out their last words: "…kingdom, and the power, and the glory, forever. Amen."

Squeezing the tears from his eyes and closing them tight, Steven Kim, the American, silently prayed.

1

NEW YORK

Saturday, May 31, 1975

"Your beginnings will seem humble, so prosperous will your future be."
—Job 8:7

Though already twenty-seven, Steven Kim felt like an excited teen as he stepped onto the tarmac at New York's Kennedy Airport. His heart was bursting with an overwhelming sense of possibility, his head swimming with American-Dream visions of unbridled prosperity. He knew some English, if not as much as he thought, and crossed to the terminal with every assurance that a bright future awaited him around the first corner.

Steven had dreamed of this moment for almost twenty years, ever since he and his classmates in South Korea had studied English as a second language in middle school. For him, the United States had always been a nation of salvation; a champion-state of equality, individualism, and democracy; a bastion of both personal and political freedom. In the late 1960s, he had gone so far as to volunteer to fight alongside American forces in Vietnam.

And the U.S. was a mostly Christian nation, Steven knew. There would even be Korean churches like the ones he'd grown up with back home, established by Korean immigrants generations before, in the early the twentieth century. In South Korea, the number of churches was increasing dramatically, and there were already more Korean Christians than there were adherents to any of the country's other religions. By this point, Steven figured, there must be tens of thousands of Korean Christians in America, and plenty of churches in New York from which to choose.

Most important for Steven, the American flag had become for him, as it had for Koreans in every walk of life, a banner of unlimited economic promise and business opportunity. For them, the U.S. was the place to go if you wanted to become rich. Wages were higher across the board, even at the lowest level, and one's earnings, he believed, in the tradition of Horatio Alger, were in direct proportion to how hard you were willing to work. It was simple *ingwa üngbo*, cause and effect, based on initiative and *poram*, worthiness. The U.S. economy was less vulnerable to market fluctuations than Korea's, and, in stark contrast to Korea's highly politicized atmosphere, family and political connections in the U.S. were not always required for commercial success. All one needed, Steven thought, were initiative and a willingness to work hard—and he was chock-full of both.

The long path that had brought him to America hadn't been easy, though. He'd been born Kim Seung-Whan to Korean parents in Seoul, South Korea, in 1949, just a year before the outbreak of the Korean War, and had grown up in a world full of violence, poverty, and hunger.

Seung-Whan's father, Kim Ki-Hong, was from Sineuju, a lumber town on the northwestern border across the Yalu River from China, and had spent his youth in the town of Sariwon. After high school, Ki-Hong went to Japan to study photography, and he later moved to China and opened a studio in Beijing, where he lived for over ten years, earning a respectable income as a well-regarded photographer.

During the Second World War, Ki-Hong joined the Chinese Army to fight the Japanese, whose brutal, genocidal occupation of Korea had lasted thirty-five years, since 1910. When the war ended, he was still relatively young, and his army service earned him the freedom of travel. He chose to return to his "liberated" homeland in the north.

Ki-Hong arrived in Sariwon expecting to help build a new, free Korean society. With the 1945 division of the once-unified country at the 38th parallel, however, he found that one occupying force—the Japanese—had been replaced by another: the Soviets. Conditions were just as repressive as they had been under Japanese rule, in some ways even worse. Many of the Soviet soldiers stationed in North Korea had been criminals and prisoners. Now, disdainful of what they saw as a subhuman foreign populace and free to act on even their grossest desires, they rampaged through the towns and countryside, taking what they liked; raping women and young girls, often in front of their parents, husbands, and children; and pillaging family homes and property. Anyone who protested their behavior was mercilessly beaten or executed on the spot.

Ki-Hong had never considered himself a communist or espoused an overtly political position, but neither had he been averse to the philosophy. Now, however, his hatred of the occupation forces caused him to despise all communists, and he did so with a vengeance, not making a distinction between Soviets and Chinese. He helped organize an underground resistance group called Young Friends against Soviet Soldiers, comprised mostly young North Koreans, whose goal was to protect the citizenry and fight against the new army of foreign invaders. Every night, they went out into the streets to search out isolated Soviet soldiers to kill and confiscate their weapons.

Ki-Hong was one of the leaders of the emerging grassroots resistance, but his position was difficult to keep secret. Other members of the community became aware of his role, and within months, an infiltrator in the Young Friends exposed him publicly and informed the Soviets of his identity. Suddenly Ki-Hong was on the run, a wanted man, facing sure execution if apprehended. Only with the help of a few trusted friends was he was able to disappear, eluding the search and, in 1946, escaping to South Korea.

When he arrived in Seoul, Ki-Hong sought out like-minded activists. Still filled with hatred for the Soviets in the north, he searched for the most anti-communist group he could find and eventually joined the influential West-North Youth League.

As he had in the north, Ki-Hong helped direct the anti-communist campaign. But he no longer needed to conduct his activities underground, since he had the support of the South Korean government. He and his fellow activists searched the country for communist sympathizers and North Korean agents. Eventually, his role was formalized, and after the war he joined the South Korean police. Now it was his job to arrest communists and send them to prison. Fluent in Korean, Chinese, and Japanese, he soon rose to the rank of detective, and he remained there until his retirement.

Ki-Hong soon met and married a South Korean woman, Hong Do-Won. And on April 17, 1949, in Seoul, the couple celebrated the birth of their first child, a son, named Seung-Whan.

One of Seung-Whan's few early or happy memories of his father was riding on the back of his motorcycle down a dusty city street. But Ki-Hong never really committed to either his wife or his child. They rarely ate or enjoyed activities as a trio, and the family didn't hold together for very long. In 1956, when Steven was six, his father left to live with another woman.

For the next six years, until Ki-Hong returned for good, Do-Won was without her husband or the benefits of his income; he didn't send them anything or stay in touch. As a single mother without other means of support, she was forced to work long hours in the nearby textile mills to keep herself and her son housed, clothed, and fed.

Ki-Hong's mother, Grandma Hong In-Sung, remained a part of their lives. A proud woman of strong Christian faith, she looked after Seung-Whan's religious upbringing, taking him to church and Sunday school every week. When he was sick, or pretending to be, he might miss school, but he never missed church; his grandmother would go so far as to carry him there on her back, if she had to. After the war, he later remembered, she would always iron paper money for him to place in the offering basket, even when times were lean.

Despite the witness of Grandma In-Sung, church was more a social opportunity than a spiritual experience for Seung-Whan. He had been born into a Christian family and had attended worship services for as long as he could remember, so he didn't feel as if there was anything more for him to learn; he just practiced without thinking. Unlike the many South Koreans who converted to Christianity during and after the war, Seung-Whan was hardly conscious of the tenets of his faith; being a Christian was just like being a member of a family, in his eyes—a birthright, not a belief. His converted friends had to learn about who Jesus was and what He had taught—for them, a whole new philosophy—but Seung-Whan never really thought about those things. They were automatic, routine.

"I didn't know Jesus Christ personally," he said years later. "'Jesus Christ— oh yeah, I believe in Jesus Christ,' I always said, but inside I didn't really know who He was."

At age fifteen, Seung-Whan sang in the church choir and helped teach Sunday school, but he wasn't moved by the services or inspired by the knowledge the ministers passed down; he didn't feel anything inside. As he grew older, he continued to tithe money to the church, but in his life outside, he did whatever he wanted, not treating Sundays—let alone any other day of the week—as God's.

Like all South Korean children, Seung-Whan learned English in school and developed a steadfast belief in "the land of the free." He pushed himself hard in his lessons and made friends with American officers serving as volunteer teachers. To him, the United States was both a land of opportunity and a refuge from communist oppression.

In the early 1960s, when the Vietnam conflict had expanded into a full-fledged battle between the U.S.-supported South Vietnamese government and the communist north, South Korea provided the second-largest contingent of foreign troops. Never having left Korea, Seung-Whan was desperate to see the world, but no one could travel abroad without fulfilling his compulsory military duty. And so, immediately upon graduating, Seung-Whan enlisted with the Korean army, along with 320,000 of his compatriots.

Despite having grown up in a war-torn land, his youthful exuberance blinded him to the dangers of fighting. As luck would have it, he landed a job in the Educational Department of the 36th Regiment of the South Korean Army's Operational Command Post, where he was tasked with preparing annual education timetables for the entire regiment. Although he was safe in his position, he was restless; he wanted to fight. Four times he applied for a transfer to combat duty, hoping to join the American forces on the ground in Vietnam. His job was vital to the regiment, though, and not everyone had the ability do it, so none of his four applications were supported or forwarded by his commanding officer. Seung-Whan was destined to serve his nation from the peaceful security of operational headquarters.

Upon completion of his term of duty, Seung-Whan returned to civilian life and decided that he wanted to go back to school. He'd always excelled in academics, and he knew that a degree could serve as a gateway to a more fulfilling life. To his disappointment, however, he wasn't able to afford the tuition, nor could he obtain a scholarship to help cover the expenses. So, he accepted a paid position as tour director with church-run cultural youth group.

Seung-Whan enjoyed his job coordinating appearances for the young performers, and it satisfied his appetite for travel, but it still wasn't what he was looking for in terms of a career. He wanted to succeed financially—to earn "real" money. This, he decided, should be his main focus. And so, after considering the best places in the world to launch a prosperous career, he weighed his options and turned his attention to his capitalist dreamland: the United States.

When Seung-Whan arrived in New York, the Korean and Vietnam wars were over, the last of the American troops having been lifted out of the chaos of Saigon just weeks earlier. The world was entering a new, modern age, based on the evidence all around him, and New York would be the center of global commerce—it was the place to be. He could hardly believe his good fortune as he set foot on U.S. soil for the first time. He had even adopted an English name to fit his new identity—Steven Kim. And he felt sure that nothing could hold him back.

Steven's most pressing challenge was money—he was practically broke. With just a few bills in his pocket and not a penny more to his name, he needed to find a job immediately, that very day. Whatever work he could find, he told himself—whatever he was offered—he would do. *I'll do anything*, he decided as he passed through customs. *If I don't work, I'll die.*

Fortunately, Steven had a contact—a high school friend who had come to the States a few years before and, like so many other Korean immigrants in New York since the beginning of the 1970s, opened a fresh produce store.

In 1960, only around four hundred Koreans lived in New York City, many of them students at Columbia University. By the end of the decade, however, Koreans had become the fastest-growing ethnic group of small-business owners in America's largest metropolitan area.

Early on, the Koreans mostly sold wigs and other Korean-made goods or subcontracted in the garment industry. Then, first in the poorer minority neighborhoods of Brooklyn, Queens, and the Bronx, Koreans began buying up grocery stores from their American owners, who were retiring at an increasing rate. They also set up shop in vacant, abandoned buildings. Many of these entrepreneurs had come from Korea with experience managing or working in small retail outfits. Now, grocery stores, produce shops, and fruit stands owned and run by recent immigrants from Korea were sprouting up weekly on almost every block and street corner in the residential districts of Manhattan. Some of these businesses operated around the clock seven days a week to take full advantage of the "City That Never Sleeps."

Without question, Steven was ready and willing to do his part. Before the sun had set on his first day in New York, he had a job selling fruit and vegetables in his family friend's produce shop in Massapequa, on Long Island, just an hour's train ride east of Manhattan.

The next morning, the owner walked Steven through the shop, pointing out bins and crates brimming with unfamiliar produce. "What's this long green thing?" Steven asked in Korean. "What do you call that red one?" He was practically bursting with questions and nervous enthusiasm. He could barely wait to start.

"You have your work cut out for you," the owner said. And he was right. But Steven didn't mind hard work. Neither did he mind getting up before dawn to prepare the store for opening, nor staying late into the night, long after the last of the evening customers had returned home, to shut it down. He quickly learned almost all of the hundreds of names for the fruits and vegetables for sale in America, and it didn't take long for his English to improve enough for him to converse comfortably with Korean and American customers alike.

2

PARTNERSHIP

*"The L*ORD *God said, 'It is not good for the man to be alone.*
I will make a helper suitable for him.'"
—Genesis 2:18

Things at the produce store were going well, and Steven quickly began adapting to the American lifestyle. He'd found a cheap apartment, which he shared with another South Korean immigrant, and his income, though not what he hoped to earn eventually, was sufficient to cover his expenses with a bit left over for savings.

After a few months, Steven's boss started questioning him about his future. "What do you want to do?" he asked him one day. "What are your plans?"

"Well, I would still like to go to school," Steven offered hesitantly, remembering his thwarted attempts in Korea to continue his education.

"Yes, yes, but after school," his boss followed. "What do you want to do after that?"

"Well, I'm not sure," he answered. "I want to make a good living, and then, one day, maybe I'll be ready to go into business on my own."

The response seemed to satisfy Steven's boss, but only temporarily. Almost the very next day, he repeated the very same questions: What were Steven's plans? What did he want to do with his future?

When the questions continued, day after day, Steven started to wonder what the man had in mind. He believed he had been a good worker, and he felt sure his boss had been satisfied with his help at the shop. Why did it seem now as if he were trying to get rid of him?

"Why do you keep asking me this?" he finally asked his boss one morning. "Is there something wrong? Am I not doing a good job? What is it that you have in mind?"

"Oh, I'm just thinking about your welfare," his boss replied. "You're doing fine here—good work, no problem. And you can probably do fine on your own, as well. But, you know," he continued, "if you marry, you'll be able to do much better."

Steven laughed to himself. So *that* was what he'd been asking about. Here, Steven had been worried there was a real problem. "Well, we'll see," he finally said. For Steven, the notion of marriage had come totally out of the blue. He had been working so hard, with his focus exclusively on earning money and making his way in America, that he hadn't given a thought to the prospect of meeting someone.

But Steven's boss was on another tack. Clearly, he had thought this marriage idea through; Steven could tell that it was no idle suggestion. And, as Steven soon found out, his boss had, in fact, already picked out a girl—a South Korean immigrant whose family he had known for years. Like the store owner, she had come with her family to the States via Argentina, and the two families had seen each other through the early days, when they'd struggled to survive.

Steven's boss assured him that the girl—who was actually a young woman in her twenties—would be perfect for him. For weeks, he kept at Steven, urging him, pushing him again and again, to at least meet her. "She's extremely smart," he said, "and very pretty, too. You can't do any better. Just let me introduce you two. No pressure. Really, I think you'll like her."

When Steven continued to decline the offer, his boss appealed to his desire for financial success. "Okay, you want to go back to school," he pointed out, "but, after you graduate, how much will you be making? This girl really knows how to earn money, how to sell things; everyone says she has a knack for it. If you marry her now, and you two work together, you'll be able to make a lot of money—much more than you ever could alone."

Steven's boss was relentless. He liked both Steven and the girl a lot and was certain the match would succeed. Not a day went by when he didn't bring up the subject and quiz Steven further. "What are you going to do?" he pushed. "What are you going to do?"

Yet, every time his boss brought up marriage or suggested he meet the girl, Steven politely declined. He had another agenda, he explained, and a girlfriend didn't fit into his plans. He wanted to be independent and make a real go of it in America—earn money, move up, and become like the business "magnates" he had seen on the covers of newsstand magazines. There'd be no settling down for Steven Kim—no girls and no distractions. Just hard work and success.

Still, Steven's boss persisted, his enthusiasm motivated less by a desire to see Steven happily hitched than the belief that if they married, the couple would work for him and, together, help him build his business into a big success. He knew the girl to be extremely sharp—a super salesperson and a smart businesswoman—and he saw in Steven a hard worker who also had good business sense.

Worn down by his boss's harangue, Steven gave in. All the buildup had made him just a little bit curious. *What kind of girl could this be?* he wondered. Could any girl really be as great as his boss said she was?

"Okay," he finally relented. "I'll take a look."

Steven's boss was overjoyed. He was pleased at having broken down Steven's defenses and thrilled at the prospect of getting the two together. Within a week, he invited the young woman and her family for a visit and told Steven to be ready. One evening after closing time, he set up a small table in the middle of the shop, with bottles of Cokes, an assortment of cookies, and a tray of nicely cut fruit.

Steven had removed his soiled apron and was pacing nervously near the back of the store. He was taken aback when the family arrived en masse—first the mother, father, and two brothers—but when the young woman entered, he stood transfixed. She had a small frame and dark, sparkling eyes that radiated warmth and intelligence. *The perfect Korean girl*, Steven thought. Just as his boss had promised.

Her name was Helen. Once everyone was introduced, everyone sat down at the table to enjoy the refreshments. Helen's parents and the shop owner recalled old friends and reminisced about their times in Argentina and Korea. Steven's boss told them how well Steven had been doing, how much more vibrant the store had been since he'd arrived.

Steven and Helen remained quiet, out of embarrassment over the arranged get-together. But, even in his awkward silence, Steven could hardly keep his eyes off of Helen, and he couldn't wait to talk with her alone. After a while, he surprised himself as much as the others when, after asking her parents' permission, he invited her to take a short walk with him.

Steven still didn't know the area very well, but he and Helen found a Friendly's ice-cream restaurant down the block and went inside. Seated across from each other in a booth, they talked over sundaes. Hesitantly at first, but then with growing comfort, they shared their backgrounds and exchanged their impressions of New York.

Helen was an only daughter, born in 1953 with the name Chang Mi An. Her parents, like Steven's, were originally from North Korea, but they had managed to escape to the south at the beginning of the war and had become successful business owners, running a cloth shop in Seoul's bustling Dongdaemun Market. They hated the violence that had claimed the life of their first son and were always afraid that another war would break out.

The 1961 coup that brought Park Chung-hee to power signaled the beginning of a massive industrialization effort in Korea as the nation moved into the global marketplace. But despite South Korea's rapidly growing economy, Park realized, there weren't sufficient internal opportunities. As an alternative, Korean families were encouraged to consider emigrating to other countries, particularly in South America. Small farmers couldn't afford to make the move, but businesspeople such as Helen's parents had sufficient finances, and so, in 1962, when Helen was nine, her parents decided that theirs would be one of the first families to leave Korea.

The first country to open its borders to Korean immigrants was Brazil. There were no direct flights available at the time, so the family had to take an arduous boat voyage by way of Hong Kong, India, and South Africa. Finally, two months after leaving Korea, the family arrived in Brazil, ready for a fresh start free from the horrors of war.

Traveling with them were a dozen prisoners of war—North Korean soldiers from detention camps in the south, set free after denouncing the Communist Party. The United Nations agreed to help them resettle, and they joined Helen's family and fourteen others in Brazil.

Even before leaving their homeland, the Koreans knew they would need land to live, and so the families had sent an advance to a Brazilian agent, trusting him to arrange a purchase for them. When they arrived, however, they found that the man had disappeared with all their money. There they were, fifteen Korean families—children and all—with no money, no land, and no place to go. For three months, they stayed in a refugee camp. Then, the Brazilian government granted them a few remote acres of virgin mountain territory. So, they started from scratch, cutting down trees and clearing the land to create arable and inhabitable plots.

Fifteen homes, as well as a chapel—Brazil's first Korean Christian Church—were built by the men, including Helen's father, who had served as elder of their church in Korea.

They plowed the earth and tried to cultivate a new crop each season, but the land they'd been given was hardly suited for farming; whatever crops they managed to grow, jungle animals would come out and eat. They tried raising chickens and ventured into the city to sell them, but that, too, proved difficult. After all, they had been business owners in Korea, not farmers. After three years of drought, crop failure, and disease, they lost everything.

The group heard that other Korean immigrants were traveling to Argentina, which offered a stronger economy and more opportunity. In 1965, desperate for another chance, they moved to Buenos Aires. Most of the children were kept out of school so that they could work and help support their parents. But Helen's parents were adamant that she receive the best education possible, and so they enrolled her at an Argentinean school, where she started in sixth grade. Providing a prosperous future for their daughter was one of the reasons they had left Korea in the first place, and they were not going to give up on that now.

Helen's parents also knew that she had a good head on her shoulders. She even began medical school—the first Korean student to attend Buenos Aires University. In 1974, her third year, her eldest brother invited the rest of the family to join him in New York. Their younger brother was already enrolled in school there, so the choice seemed clear—the family was moving again.

In New York, Helen went to work selling general merchandise for a small, Argentinean-owned department store, the Mar Company, on 30th Street in Manhattan. She had a talent for sales and excelled in the business, quickly becoming the company's top salesperson. Although Korean was probably her weakest language, she spoke several others, and her fluency in Spanish was a great advantage, as the business catered mainly to South American buyers looking to purchase electronics in the U.S. to resell in their home countries. The only thing left for Helen, according to her parents, was to find a suitable husband.

Right from the start, Helen and Steven communicated easily, and their sheer excitement over meeting each other kept the conversation flowing. Again, Helen's command of Korean was not strong, since she had left the country as a young child, but her English was passable. And so, speaking in Steven's second language, they shared their hopes and dreams for a better life. Helen liked Steven's smile; she found him nice in a respectful sort of way. Steven liked everything about Helen. In short they hit it off immediately— Steven's resistance to his boss's matchmaking had melted as soon as she'd walked into the shop.

Even though Steven was geographically distant from his family in Korea, they were still a central part of his life and plans—his mother, especially. He had been glad to meet Helen's parents, and, after just one encounter, he wanted his parents to meet Helen, as well. He wanted to show her off, and he knew they would approve. But Korea was so far away. What could he do? Then, it came to him: He suggested to Helen that they have their picture taken at a professional studio and send it for his parents to see.

There was a camera store near the shop, Steven told her, with a photography studio in the rear. Helen laughed at the spontaneity of his proposal. It was a rather bold move, but she agreed. They rushed to the studio, posed together for a portrait, and returned to the fruit shop, all smiles, to let everyone know.

"What did you do?" Helen's father scolded her. "On the first date? You don't even know him!" Clearly, he was not entirely pleased. Then again, neither was he really as angry as he let on. He had been impressed by the shop owner's reports about Steven, who seemed like a promising young man; and, after all, his daughter was no longer in her teens.

From there, the relationship flourished. Over the next several months, the couple spent most of their free time together, and the following September, having secured the approval of both families, they announced their engagement.

Steven's boss had kept a close eye on their courtship, constantly questioning Steven about his intentions. He had been overjoyed to hear that the couple was to be wed and felt proud to have conceived of the match and introduced them. It seemed that he believed his own efforts and foresight were the reason they'd found each other. And now, he began pushing his own agenda. He suggested to Steven—gently at first, and more vigorously as time progressed—that Helen join the business. "After you marry, what are you going to do?" he asked.

"Well, I don't want to be a country boy," Steven replied. Massapequa was in the suburbs; it wasn't really New York. "At least one of us needs to work in the city. New York is a big international place, and I want to have a feel for what's happening in the outside world. I have my own life, Helen has hers, and then we share one together. I don't want both of us to work in one place. I hope you understand."

He didn't. Marry, live together, work together—those were his plans for the young couple. "I want you and Helen to work with me," he insisted. "I need you to make this business grow. It can be a huge success, but only with you both."

But Steven didn't give in. Even though his original vision had been altered the day he'd met Helen, he was determined to follow his dream of working for his own success—not someone else's.

His boss was furious. He had taken a risk on Steven by investing time and energy initiating him in American commerce. He had given him a job, introduced him to Helen, and spoken on his behalf. And what kind of thanks did he get? Just when he needed Steven—and Helen—the most, they were turning their backs on him.

He couldn't just sit by idly and let it happen. Driven by apparent anger, disappointment, and selfish greed, he told Helen's family that he had made a huge mistake. He'd thought that Steven was a good and honest person, but, in fact, he didn't know as much about Steven's family as he had let on, and he was starting to realize that Steven's past was not as spotless as he had presented it to be. Worse yet, he told them that he had recently discovered that Steven had been keeping a second girlfriend on the side. He apologized profusely for his poor judgment and for not having checked Steven's background properly. He even offered to help Helen's family pay for the engagement expenses once the wedding was called off.

Naturally, Helen's parents were disturbed by the "news." They had welcomed the news of Helen's engagement to Steven, but now they thought it was based on false impressions and pressured her to break it off.

Steven had no idea that any of this was happening. As far as he was concerned, everything was going great. He loved Helen; their engagement was progressing nicely; and they would soon be wed. His boss had been rather brusque ever since Steven had turned down his proposition that Helen join them in the business, but otherwise, everything was fine.

Then, one morning, while Steven was sorting oranges into bins, his boss called him over, saying there was a phone call for him.

Steven picked up the receiver and heard Helen's voice. She had been wanting to talk to him, she said. She'd thought things over and decided that she wanted to go back to school. She had done well at the university in Argentina and hoped to continue her education. She was sorry, she said, but she couldn't marry him right then; the timing just wasn't right. She didn't say a word about his boss's reports or about how devastated she had been to hear that her fiancé had been seeing someone else and lying to her all along.

"Education—that's great," Steven replied, unfazed. "You go to school. I'll wait for you." All he knew was that he loved Helen and he wasn't about to lose her. He was more than willing to wait as long as he had to, and to do whatever he needed, if it meant they would be together.

"I don't know," she said. "These things can be very difficult. I don't know how long it might take. Maybe we should just hold off and see what happens."

As it turned out, Steven didn't have to wait very long. In a fit of parental protectiveness, Helen's father had written to Korea, asking his brother-in-law, who was a member of the Korean equivalent of the CIA, to perform a thorough vetting of his daughter's suitor. They ran a full background check on Steven and his family.

At the same time, a former high school classmate of Steven's who lived in Argentina contacted Helen's father. Everyone gave the same, glowing report: Steven was intelligent and hardworking—an enterprising young man bound for success.

Helen's father relented; the engagement was back on.

In a little over a year spent working in America, Steven had built a nest egg of almost $10,000—a considerable amount of money for a young couple. He and Helen discussed the prospect of buying a store and going into business on their own; they probably had enough resources to get it started. However, Steven was young and somewhat impulsive, and his love for Helen brought out his less practical side. They were starting a new life together, and he wanted to do it right. He treated his bride-to-be lavishly, buying her diamond rings and a beautiful Rolex watch. Whatever she needed or just wanted, he bought.

In a matter of months, Steven had spent the bulk of his savings; the little that remained, he gave to Helen's mother to help cover the cost of the wedding. Financially, he was right back where he had started—with nothing—but he didn't care one bit. He was about to marry the love of his life.

Steven and Helen were wed December 18, 1976. At their reception, they were given a great amount in monetary gifts, as is the Korean custom. But that money, too, went toward their celebration—the newlyweds enjoyed a classic Hawaiian honeymoon.

Steven's boss, still seething over the rejection of his offer and now shamed by the exposure of his backstabbing lies, fired Steven the very day the couple returned from Hawaii. And so, Steven and Helen began their new life together as husband and wife with almost as little in savings as he'd had in his pocket when he'd first arrived in New York. Between them, they had only $200 in cash.

Ever a hard worker, Steven had no trouble securing a new job at another produce shop, and soon he was bringing home a modest $150 a week. And Helen, drawing on her valuable experience and sales genius working for an electronic export business, obtained a sales management position in midtown Manhattan. When the store owner offered their salespeople the incentive of higher commissions to move outdated inventory, she jumped at the chance to increase her earnings. As soon as a customer entered the store, Helen would immediately guide him or her to the older merchandise, with an enthusiastic explanation as to why it was a better value—less expensive and just as good. Before long, she was bringing in several times Steven's income—her base wages plus another $500 a week in commissions.

In three years, Steven and Helen saved enough to buy a house on Long Island, and it wasn't long before they had three children: Eric, Lisa, and Charles. Steven's vision on the tarmac at Kennedy Airport had come true—he and Helen were living the American Dream.

Eventually, true to their plans, the couple went into business for themselves, partnering with Helen's parents to set up their own produce operation, Victory Fruit, in Bay Ridge, Brooklyn.

Running his own store was demanding, but Steven was undaunted, and determined, as always, to succeed in business by working harder than anyone else. He awoke every morning at one o'clock and drove a truck to the New York City Produce Market at Hunts Point in the South Bronx. A sixty-acre enterprise with 700,000 square feet of refrigerated storage, it was the largest wholesale produce market in the world, serving produce sellers throughout the New York metropolitan area.

The market was always hopping. It was five or six before most of the store owners arrived to do their shopping, but Steven knew that the earliest buyers had the best selection to choose from. And so, he made sure to be among the one or two hundred grocers—out of the thousands who shopped at Hunts Point—who arrived early, in order to stock the highest quality of produce. Well before dawn, he would search through crate after crate for the freshest, ripest fruit and vegetables. This practice attracted a base of loyal customers, many of whom traveled as far as twenty or thirty blocks to buy from the high-end stock of his store—a selection as good as anywhere else in New York.

By three in the morning, Steven had selected his produce and loaded the truck, which he then drove back to Bay Ridge to unload, filling bins and arranging stacks of fruits and vegetables. If he completed this task within a couple of hours, he would go back to bed for a few more winks of sleep—ninety minutes max—before the store opened, at seven. This was his morning routine, six days a week. But he couldn't complain; the money was good, and that was the point, after all.

In the meantime, Helen returned to the electronics export business in Manhattan, where she not only distinguished herself as top salesperson but also started helping her brother run the company. With her linguistic abilities and natural affinity for people, she had excellent interpersonal skills, and her customers quickly learned they could count on her for the best quality products at the lowest prices. She soon expanded the company's product line to feature more electronics and home appliances, including high-end Japanese brands, such as Sony and Panasonic, and sales were booming.

3

AMERICAN DREAMING

*"Then the land will yield its fruit,
and you will eat your fill and live there in safety."*
—Leviticus 25:19

For the next three years, both of the couple's businesses did extraordinarily well. When the long hours began to wear on Steven, Helen suggested that he switch industries and join her and her brother in the export business.

Steven agreed, and with the money they had saved from the produce business, combined with Helen's earnings, they bought a half interest in the Argentinean store. Steven was put in charge of the electronics department, while Helen and her brother managed overall operations. The business kept growing—at its peak, it brought in over $50,000 daily. Within the year, the three bought it outright.

They also discussed establishing a new venture of their own. A friend of Steven's had recently put his furniture business up for sale. The investment capital of $50,000 posed no problem for the prospering couple, and the idea appealed to Steven's entrepreneurial spirit. So, they bought it—and it prospered, as well.

But Steven had become a restless capitalist, and owning one store was no longer enough. It wasn't so much for the money, even though that was good; it was for the challenge—Steven thrived on it. So, he kept upping the ante. He opened a second store, and a third, each addition increasing the volume, the profits, and the challenge.

Increased sales and a changing, expanding customer base demanded new products—and more of them. Steven started taking trips abroad, first to Korea and then elsewhere, to purchase furniture at wholesale prices to import to the States. He kept buying more and more merchandise; there seemed to be no limit to how much product he could bring in or how fast he could move it out. His determination to buy and sell—to increase sales and profit—became insatiable.

Eventually—perhaps inevitably—Steven's purchases surpassed the stores' capacity. Their customer base was growing at a slower rate than he was expanding the variety and quantity of his product lines, and the inventory started backing up. The business had reached a dangerous precipice, with much of their capital locked up in stock he couldn't move.

The warehouse was filled to capacity. Somehow, Steven had to increase his sales volume—but how? He had three retail stores, but the options they afforded him were limited. The logical, seemingly obvious, solution was to ratchet up his whole operation and sell the merchandise wholesale.

Steven knew the principles behind such a move, and he also realized he couldn't pull it off alone. He hired a full managerial staff of experienced, knowledgeable merchandising professionals and prepared to do business at a new, corporate level. When he'd started out in the grocery business, he had traveled to the biggest market to find the best, freshest produce at the lowest prices. Now, he needed to become the biggest market. To sell his merchandise wholesale, he had to become the furniture equivalent of the market at Hunts Point.

What he found was a market that sounded almost identical, even in name. In North Carolina, near Greensboro, the High Point Furniture Market had been in operation for over a hundred and fifty years, since the late nineteenth century. It had begun as a factory, Steven learned, but had quickly evolved into a retail operation and then a wholesale market for a wide range of manufacturers and importers, showing steady growth and diversification in the field. With millions of square feet of showrooms, the High Point Market attracted tens of thousands of visitors and potential buyers. It had become a dominant force in both the American and international furniture markets and also boasted the largest furnishings trade show in the world.

The High Point exhibition had recently been consolidated into a semiannual event, taking place in April and October. Steven and his staff prepared feverishly for the first show. They rented a space in the enormous pavilion and showcased their best lines in beautiful displays, with prices marked as low as possible.

Buyers were attracted almost immediately by the combination of quality products and reasonable prices. Steven was a quick learner, and his years of experience purchasing merchandise overseas and selling it to retail customers gave him an advantage over many of the other wholesalers—he had a clear sense of what people wanted. Just as important, he held the retailers' interest by listening and responding to their particular preferences and desires.

Sooner than expected, Steven and Helen found that their inventory was flowing smoothly once again, and they were making more than they had ever dreamed of. Within months, money was practically no object; whenever they needed more, it came. And as soon as it did, they would reinvest it, buying more, selling more, and increasing every day. Banks were practically banging on their doors to lend them whatever funds they required, and merchandise flowed in and out more freely than ever. At any given moment, there was hardly any cash on hand, but it was always readily available, and before they knew it, their business was worth millions.

Helen's brother, too, saw his holdings multiply many times over. And, as was true for Steven, the more money he showed on the books, the more the banks were willing to lend him—at irresistible rates. He invested in stocks and real estate—at the height of the boom, he owned eight Manhattan office buildings worth tens of millions of dollars. The market kept rising, and Steven, Helen, and her family—practically anyone who had sufficient collateral off of which to borrow or a few dollars to invest—kept getting richer. It seemed that the good times would never end.

But the bubble finally burst. On October 19, 1987—the day that would become known as "Black Monday"—the Dow Jones average dropped by more than five hundred points, or almost 25 percent of the market's value. It was the largest single-day decline in history. Financial markets around the world plummeted, losing as much as half their value in Asia. Many companies couldn't weather the shock or make up for the loss of available funds; they went under. And even those that survived took a huge hit.

Overnight, those who had speculated during the 1980s buying frenzy saw their portfolios reduced to almost nothing. Privately owned businesses like Steven and Helen's, which relied on a dynamic balance of income and loans, were especially hard-hit.

When the floor of the market fell out from under them, Steven had been running the furniture business, Helen the electronics import-export business in Manhattan. Within a month, both ventures failed. The couple, as well as her brother and family, lost everything—businesses, equity, stocks, real estate, and whatever money they had invested in other enterprises.

Saddled with debt, yet without a business to generate income, Steven and Helen were back where they started once again. Steven was neither humbled nor worried, however; in fact, he was even somewhat excited to take on this new challenge. Together, he and Helen had made it through hard times before, he reminded her— they had turned a few dollars into millions—and he had known since his first talk with her over ice cream at Friendly's that Helen was not a woman to accept defeat without a fight. Her creative intelligence and commercial ingenuity had always served her well. Almost immediately, they were discussing new concepts, and in a couple of days, Helen had another business venture in mind.

All that remained from their furniture business were some catalogs from the companies they had dealt with—about fifty in total. Spotting one on the floor of their home office, Helen said, "I just need one good catalog."

"Why?" Steven asked.

"For a start," she said, "to get us going. Find a good one—and cheap."

So, they rummaged through stacks of catalogs, searching for the one that would turn around their fortunes. And there, buried in the remnants of the failed business's paperwork, Steven found a catalog from a Canadian store that sold bedroom furniture.

Next, using her winsome personality and the skills of persuasion she had honed over the years, Helen somehow convinced a landlord to lease them a small space in a newly constructed commercial building in Flushing, Queens. They didn't have the money to pay the rent, but she negotiated the security deposit and the first two months' rent with a post-dated check.

There was just enough money left in their personal accounts to purchase one bedroom set. "Order it," she told Steven. It wasn't much, but, she repeated, it was all they needed—a start.

In the weeks that followed, Steven and Helen constructed a basic show-room to display the single bedroom set, made some phone calls to friends and former customers, and began taking orders. Within a month, they had made $50,000 in sales—a profit of over $20,000—by keeping just one set in stock at a time and purchasing new merchandise as needed. Already, they were able to pay off their outstanding debts, with enough left over to move the business forward.

"It was amazing," Steven remembered years later. "Just like Helen said, from that small start, the business just took off." At first, they sold retail, but Steven knew from experience that the real money was either in furniture manufacturing or in buying it cheaply overseas and selling it wholesale. And to do that, they needed more inventory.

Steven and Helen's contacts in South Korea came in handy. They reached an agreement with a set of Korean producers and immediately started import-ing merchandise from the Korean market. Their business did well, in part because of a rapidly expanding Korean manufacturing base. With the founda-tion of trust that they had built with Korean businesses, the couple was able to purchase furniture in bulk and on credit.

As the Korean economy grew, so, too, did its currency. Changes in mon-etary policy and general economic conditions, particularly the tremendous boost from the 1988 Olympic Games in Seoul, created an economic boom in the late 1980s. The Games drew the greatest number of participants in

Olympic history, with South Korea realizing a profit of nearly five hundred million dollars. Reversing its previously steady devaluation against the U.S. dollar, the Korean *won* rose more than 25 percent in the latter half of the decade, with significant increases every year. With the drastic shift in the comparative value of national currencies, American buyers were being priced out of the Korean market.

"This is the end of it," Steven realized when he first saw their profit margins dwindling. They needed another source.

At the 1987 convention of the National Office Products Association, in Chicago, Steven met Charles Leung, a Chinese businessman from Hong Kong. The two men hit it off. They were about the same age, and Charles, too, had suffered a series of recent setbacks in his business. That very year, it had been announced that the sovereignty of Hong Kong be transferred back to Mainland China in ten years' time. Investors became nervous about the financial future of Hong Kong, and spending slowed to a standstill. As a result, Charles's sources of funding had frozen up—no one wanted to invest any money. All ten of his businesses were going under, if they hadn't already done so. Like Steven, Charles had made and lost millions, and had come to the Chicago convention looking for new business.

The two men talked throughout the day, sharing their common woes. That evening, they went to a Korean restaurant and continued their conversation over drinks and dinner. After dessert, the waiter brought them another round of drinks, and Charles had a brainstorm. "Let's go to China together," he suggested. "We'll start over again—kill them dead.

"China is just now opening to American businesses," Charles explained. "It's the perfect time to get in on the ground floor. I'm living in Hong Kong and know how things run over there. I can set up a factory in China in no time. You have experience with the American wholesale market and High Point; you have long-standing relationships with American buyers. And, most importantly, we both know the furniture business inside out.

"With my loss of financial backers, my retail shops in Hong Kong are about to go belly-up. I need to start something new. You've lost your Korean manufacturing connections and have to find a new source of merchandise. Come on; why don't we go start something together and see what we can do?"

Steven had never been to Hong Kong, or anywhere else in China, and he didn't speak a word of Chinese. But what Charles was saying made sense—business sense. Charles, he had learned, knew how to produce Italian-style lacquer chairs, and in China they could cut their manufacturing costs to a fraction of what either of them had paid in the past. And the chairs, he knew, would be a sure seller in the U.S.

"Yeah, why don't we?" he finally agreed.

"That," Steven remembered later, "is how it all started."

4

NOVEMBER 1987

Guangzhou, China

*"So neither he who plants nor he who waters is anything, but only God,
who makes things grow."*
—1 Corinthians 3:7

For Steven, going to China was just a sales venture, another way to make money. Helen had immediately recognized the sales potential in Charles's proposal and was supportive from the start. Steven would base himself on Long Island and fly to China when it was required by the business. She did set one rule: He couldn't be away from home for more than fifteen days at a time.

First, Steven needed an American visa. Although he was a resident of the U.S., he remained a citizen of South Korea. Visa issues had never been a problem for his past travels, but this was different—China and South Korea didn't recognize each other diplomatically, and the Korean government forbade its citizens from traveling to communist countries, especially China. There was only one solution. After the usual delays and bureaucratic hang-ups, Steven finally became an American citizen in the summer of 1987.

A few months later, Steven and Charles arrived by boat at the southern seaport of Guangzhou, just seventy-five miles northwest of Hong Kong. With a metropolitan population of nearly ten million, Guangzhou was the most populous city in Guangdong Province and the third largest in China. Of even greater relevance, it was the economic center of the Pearl River Delta, one of China's leading commercial and manufacturing regions.

Steven's first impression of Guangzhou was that it was full of dust. Even the areas that had been beautifully landscaped with manicured trees and flowering shrubs were covered with oily soot. Still, he recognized that the region was the perfect place to set up business.

As Steven would find in most of China's southern provinces, Guangdong's residents were friendly and more than willing to do business with him; China wanted desperately to enter into the global market. The country had yet to attract many foreign business partners or investors, and the market was still wide open. There were many garage-like workplaces in Guangdong, but overall, the area's industrial facilities were significantly underused, and many of the big factories were practically abandoned. Valuable equipment often sat dormant. Setting up a factory was very inexpensive—labor was dirt cheap and abundant, as was the wood to make furniture. In no time, the partners were in business as C & E Enterprises, manufacturing chairs in China and shipping them to the U.S.

The success of their business was based on the fact that these were no ordinary chairs but high-quality, high-gloss, lacquered Italian knockoffs. No one in China had ever seen them before, and no one else knew how to make them.

Charles brought several models from Italy, and by the fall of 1988, Steven took half a dozen cheaply manufactured samples to New York. The salesmen and wholesale buyers he invited to C & E's New York showroom responded with unanimous enthusiasm: they loved the chairs' glossy style and especially appreciated the quality of the merchandise, making a favorable comparison with the high-end Hong-Kong-produced furniture they were accustomed to. When they discovered that the chairs had been made in mainland China, they scrutinized the samples for defects, turning the chairs upside down and testing all the joints. They were amazed when they discovered no flaws.

The winning factor, as Charles and Steven had anticipated, was the recommended selling price—$60, or half of what the wholesalers would have had to pay for the original chairs, from Italy. This meant a profit of 100 percent for the wholesalers. And C & E was the exclusive supplier.

The buyers snapped up the entire first line, and the Italian-style chairs quickly became such a sensation in the American furniture market that Steven and Charles could hardly keep up with the demand for them. C & E developed a Western division, managed by Charles's sister, and production kept increasing, especially with the rapid growth of the High Point Market: 55,000 people attended the 1989 exposition—almost double the attendance from earlier in the decade—and the exhibition showrooms were expanded by three million square feet.

Over the next ten years, Charles and Steven sold millions of chairs and earned tens of millions of dollars in profit. Steven became known as the "Chair King." He traveled to China half a dozen times a year to maintain the flow of chairs to the States, and every time he stayed away for his maximum allowance of fifteen days. He traveled constantly to China and back, coming home for three weeks or a month at a time before heading over again. Much like when he'd worked day and night selling produce, Steven's life revolved around his business.

Helen accompanied Steven to China only once. She didn't much like China, she complained, and she was especially unhappy with the accommodations. South Korea was not on par with American standards of cleanliness, but China was far worse. She and Steven stayed at a first-class hotel, and she refused to use the facilities anywhere else; even if they were visiting a market or a factory, she insisted on taking a taxi back to the hotel to use the restroom or even simply to wash her hands. One trip was more than enough, and she declared that she would never again go to China with Steven.

Without Helen by his side, Steven's life in China became almost like a bachelor's. He rented a duplex in a six-story apartment building in Chang'an, setting up an office on the third floor, with his living quarters above.

Steven never learned to read Chinese, and he used interpreters when negotiating business transactions. But he and Charles knew enough of the language to get around. At night, they would go for drinks at karaoke bars and private men's clubs, or take jaunts to Beijing. As wealthy businessmen, they never wanted for women more than willing to keep them company.

Little by little, Steven lengthened the duration of his trips, to the point where he would stay in China for a couple of months at a time and return to the U.S. for only a brief visit, occurring about six times a year. Business was booming, he was enjoying himself, and it seemed that the good times would never end.

The partners couldn't keep their success a secret, however, and around 1993, others in the furniture trade zeroed in on their product. Chinese investors and manufacturers visited their factory to examine the operation, then sent friends and relatives to work there and pick up the manufacturing techniques. Six to eight months later, they would open their own factories nearby and manufacture basically the same chairs, but for ten to fifteen dollars apiece—priced low enough to undercut Charles and Steven's business.

Soon the market was flooded with imitations of C & E's imitations. Charles and Steven tried lowering their prices to keep pace with the competition, but their profit margin became so slim that they couldn't maintain production. They tried moving their factory to another area and producing lower-end merchandise; they even sold shares on the public market to raise funds for a corporate reorganization. But when they failed to show sufficient profit, C & E's stock plummeted, and the partners could no longer keep the company viable. On New Year's Day of 1994, Charles called Steven from Hong Kong to let him know that it was all gone; a new investor had taken over the business.

Neither Steven nor Charles was the type to give up easily. The two traveled deeper into the countryside of southern China to scope out new manufacturing opportunities. Business was still booming in the region, and possibilities abounded. For a while, they sold marble dining tables to Macy's and other American department stores, but the stone proved brittle in transit and difficult to handle for untrained workers.

They tried making home-assembly chairs for Walmart, but many customers returned the units they had purchased after having problems putting them together. When Walmart demanded refunds and credit, Steven warned Charles that there was a problem in the way the chair parts had been manufactured, but Charles disagreed and refused to make the necessary changes. They argued, and Steven ultimately resigned from the corporation, effectively ending their ten-year partnership.

In 1997, Steven left the manufacturing industry, joined with another partner, and became a merchandiser, buying for a catalog house in St. Louis. Instead of managing the factory work directly, he would send designs from the States to China, where a factory would produce samples, and then, after the designs had been refined and the prices set, he would arrange all the transactions and shipments. As a middleman, he was spared having to deal with the many challenges on the manufacturing side of the business, as well as the difficulties of managing Chinese workers.

By the second year in his new career, Steven was shipping almost five hundred containers annually. His business continued to prosper until 1999, when he got greedy—without informing his partner or their buyer, Steven raised his commission from the manufacturers and skimmed off the difference to woo his own buyers; the remaining money he spent lavishly on entertainment. When one of his employees blew the lid off of his scheme, Steven lost both his supplier and his primary buyer. He was also threatened with a lawsuit and forced to resign. Yet another of Steven's business ventures had gone under.

5

MAY 1999

Shenzhen

"Ask and it will be given to you; seek and you will find;
knock and the door will be opened to you."
—Matthew 7:7

*O*nce again, Steven was out of work and on his own. But, this time, he wasn't without resources—he still had the merchandising end of the business down pat, along with clients whose loyalty he had earned by dint of hard work and consistent results. Yet, after years of partnership, it was a challenge to go back into business by himself. In China, without Helen by his side, he'd lost a portion of self-confidence. He wasn't sure what to do, and, for the first time since Helen had opened that Canadian furniture catalog and launched a business venture, Steven began having doubts that compelled him to reflect on his career and rethink his life.

For so many years, he had been living to earn. His only purpose in coming to China had been to get rich. He had worked hard, not caring about anything else, and earned millions in the process. He'd lost millions and then earned them back again, only to lose them once more. It seemed like an endless cycle. He felt as if he was trapped in a hamster cage, running as fast as he could to keep the wheel spinning yet always remaining in the same place. *Is that all there is?* he asked himself. Some part of him wanted more. In the course of pursuit of success, he had lost sense of where he had come from, of who he was.

I'm a Christian, Steven considered. *Maybe God wants to me to involve Him more in my life.*

Steven did venture back into business, buying again from regional factories and selling to several former clients and some new ones, too. Only this time, he started taking his faith more seriously. He didn't know of any Korean churches, but on Sundays, he would take a boat to Hong Kong to worship and then return to Chang'an in the afternoon.

One Sunday, Steven thought, *Today is our day of worship; I should go to church.* But he was prevented from traveling to Hong Kong by an appointment he'd scheduled for the early evening. Later that day, traveling by car to the factory where the meeting was to take place, he passed what he thought was a new building. "All of a sudden, there was a church right in front of me," he later described. "So I shouted to the driver, 'Stop! Stop!' It was a beautiful church building with a big cross. I had never seen such a church in China."

Looking closer, Steven saw that the building was indeed a Chinese church. Somehow he had never noticed it before. He went inside and asked a man in the entrance hall, "Do you know if there are any Korean churches around here?"

"Yes," the man replied. "It's right upstairs."

"Really?" Steven responded. Without another word, he bounded up a set of side steps. Sure enough, on the fourth floor, there it was—a Korean-Chinese church! He could hardly believe his eyes.

Near the top of the stairs, a man was sweeping. "When are the services?" Steven asked him, still amazed.

"Oh, I'm sorry," the man said. "They were at two. They're already over; everyone is gone now."

"Bad luck," Steven said, disappointed. "Will there be services next week?"

"Oh, yes," the man replied. "Every Sunday, two o'clock."

Steven came back to the church for the Korean service the following Sunday—and the Sunday after that, and the one after that. He kept attending for the next couple of months, relieved to have found an outlet for his faith.

Despite Steven's initial enthusiasm, he still wasn't completely happy; he soon fell into the same old pattern of mechanical worship. He wasn't making a spiritual connection, and he thought he knew why.

Several parishioners were migrant Korean-Chinese workers with menial jobs—or no job at all. If they paid the equivalent of $25 a month, Steven had found out, the church provided them with room and board, the only condition being that they attend church services. As a result, although more than a hundred young people filled the pews, sang, and followed along at the services, they did so without real spiritual commitment. Steven could sense the difference; nothing felt natural. It was all set up like a commercial exchange—their attendance for something to eat and a place to sleep. It was nothing like what he had been used to back in the States.

Well, at least there are some Koreans here, Steven thought. Over the course of his ten years in China, he had hardly met any Koreans. Seeing them reminded him of all the things he missed about his native culture—the food, in particular. He hadn't been to New York in a while, and he missed Helen's cooking.

Steven had an idea. Maybe he could find someone from the congregation who could cook for his office. That way, he and his staff wouldn't have to order out all the time, and they could enjoy the authentic Korean fare they all craved. He asked around at church and finally hired an older Korean woman to work part-time cooking at his office.

In her first week on the job, the new cook mentioned to Steven that she also worked for another Korean businessman who attended a Christian church.

"Which one?" Steven asked.

"Oh, the Korean church in Shenzhen," she replied. "You know, the one by the factories."

A Korean church? Steven was definitely interested.

Officially, China accepted four religions: Buddhism, Taoism, Islam, and Christianity, which it divided into Catholicism and Protestantism. Article 36 of the Constitution of the People's Republic of China even stipulated that "[c]itizens…enjoy freedom of religious belief" and that "[n]o State organ, public organization, or individual may compel citizens to believe in, or not to believe in, any religion; nor may they discriminate against citizens who believe in, or do not believe in, any religion."

In conflict with this public policy, however, the Communist Party was officially atheist and stated explicitly that Party membership and religious belief were not compatible. Foreign and unrecognized religious groups were strictly forbidden, and even those that had been granted official recognition had to report to the local Party authorities, whose consent was required before any meetings were organized. Once a group filed a report, they essentially placed themselves under government control, subjecting themselves to constant surveillance. They could not evangelize to people under eighteen, and they could not allow any illegal foreign nationals, especially North Koreans, to attend their services.

As a rule, therefore, most Korean churches didn't register with the government. Instead, they operated illegally and stayed underground, which explained why Steven had not been aware of any in the region.

The "church" his cook had told him about in Shenzhen turned out to be just such a congregation—a group of Korean Christians who gathered secretly every Sunday in a rented hotel ballroom. They were a legitimate Korean church, but, to mask their activities, they billed their organization as the Korean Cultural Association, without any overt religious affiliation.

Despite the church's mundane front, Steven found the worship to be both serious and spiritual. In Shenzhen, he'd discovered the exact type of Christian worship which he'd been searching for.

Shenzhen City was a protected economic zone, off-limits to outside Chinese workers. It was a forty-five-minute drive from Steven's apartment in

Chang'an, and to get there, he had to pass through a police checkpoint. As a foreign businessman with a valid passport, however, he didn't have any trouble. Every morning, he would drive to the church for an early prayer meeting, then return to Chang'an in time for the day's work.

When Steven first started worshipping at the Shenzhen hotel services, there were usually sixty or seventy Koreans in attendance. The following month, when he returned from a trip to New York for Thanksgiving, that number had been cut in half. There had been a rift in the church, someone told him; some of the parishioners hadn't liked how the preacher was handling things, and so they had left. The Cultural Association was in trouble, the person said—in danger of disbanding. It needed to revive its congregation. What the church really needed, Steven saw, was new leadership.

He didn't have to wait long. The very next month, a new pastor did arrive—two pastors, actually. They were a Korean husband-and-wife missionary team.

The congregation didn't increase immediately, but the advent of pastors Won and Cho was an inspiration for Steven and many of the members who had remained. At first, the wife, Pastor Cho, was very quiet; she mostly just prayed. Yet Steven was startled, even moved, by the quality of her prayers—by her fervency, which often brought her to tears. It seemed to him that her devotions were all that mattered to her—the center of her life. What a difference from his own life, he thought. And that was just what he had wanted to work on.

One of the first things the new pastors did was begin a Bible study group. They asked the participants to engage in a daily practice—what they called "quiet time"—with the Bible. Steven had never done this before. Thankfully, Pastor Won provided instructions: first, pray; then, sing; then, read; and then, when a word or a sentence stuck out, underline it and meditate on it more deeply. Finally, he instructed them to find a way to apply the results of their meditation to their daily lives. The goal was to do this every day.

Steven found that the self-control required to observe a daily quiet time was difficult, but he was determined to stay with it. At first, he was faithful, but it wasn't long before he was missing a day here and there. A few months into the practice, however, he started to get the hang of the process; after that, he never missed a single session. Before long, the discipline became the anchor of his spiritual life. Just as Pastor Won had promised, he felt like he was actu-ally getting deeper into the text, seeing the words from the inside.

Pastors Won and Cho gave Steven just the impetus he needed to revive his spiritual devotions. He read through the whole Bible with them and joined their vibrant prayer group. "We studied together and worshipped together," he remembered years later. "They became my guides and mentors in spiritual life, leading and guiding me from the very beginning. I had always been a Christian and had even been becoming more active, but I felt like I had never met Jesus personally. I hadn't actually realized the depths of meaning in the term 'the living God.'"

On Sundays, Steven, as the church's membership director, would sit at one of the communal lunch tables after the service and welcome the new-comers, introducing them to the other worshippers and encouraging them to return the following week.

As Steven progressed, pastors Won and Cho gave him the opportunity to lead a small Bible study group. He would take notes during his sessions with the pastors and then share what he had learned with the members of his own group. Learning and teaching, teaching and learning—this is how he developed. He had heard it said that the best way to learn was to teach, and he could hardly tell which role taught him more: student or teacher. Soon, he became a deacon—a lay minister—and began preaching.

Even with all of his growth and spiritual maturity, Steven realized that he still had a long way to go. When he inquired about the prayer habits of the members of his Bible study group, one man said that he prayed in the morning.

"For how long?" Steven asked him.

"An hour or two," the man replied. If you were a minister, he had learned, you should pray at least three hours a day—for a layperson, at least one.

Steven stopped, silent. Although he had benefited tremendously from the inspiration and training of pastors Won and Cho, he had still been struggling to pray for even fifteen or twenty minutes at a time. He knew he had a lot of room left for improvement.

6

JULY 2000

Father School

*"Husbands, love your wives, just as Christ loved the church
and gave himself up for her to make her holy, cleansing her
by the washing with water through the word."*
—Ephesians 5:25–26

During Steven's studies with pastors Won and Cho, they sometimes talked about something called Father School. Pastor Won said that it was like Promise Keepers—a mission based in America that focused on helping men become more devoted Christians, through their commitment to their families, and more devoted fathers and husbands, through their commitment to Christ.

If the father of a family stood tall in his faith, Won explained—if he was spiritually strong—his family would stand tall, as well. The purpose of Father

School was to strengthen the faith of the whole family by training the father to lead them.

"Any man can become a father," Pastor Won told the men in the group. "All you have to do is have children. Some men don't even marry; it's no real accomplishment. But, in the Bible, the father, following our heavenly Father, serves a critical role. And because we have forgotten our Father, we have forgotten that we, too, are fathers with responsibilities and sacred missions.

"Our Father has blessed us," he told them. "And we, in turn, should bless our wives and our children. That is our job, given to us by God. After all, if you don't bless your children, who will? You are the ones who have to be responsible."

Pastor Won's words struck Steven like a thunderbolt. He had been in China a long time. But what about Helen and their children? At first, he had been based in New York, traveling to China only when needed and never leaving home for more than fifteen consecutive days. Over time, however, his stints in China had lengthened, until the days he spent there outnumbered those spent at home in the U.S. For ten years, he had essentially been based in China, making the occasional trip to New York. He had been neglectful, he realized, caring more about himself and his business than about his wife and

Steven and Helen enjoy a Caribbean cruise in 2001 during one of Steven's rare trips home.

children. He had always told his family that he wanted to earn money in order to improve their lives. In his heart, he'd known all along that this wasn't the whole truth. And he knew they had suffered.

Five years earlier, in 1995, their eldest son, Eric, had gone away to college. At first, everything had seemed fine. Some weeks later, Steven, in Chang'an, had gotten a call saying that Eric was having trouble. Steven had flown to New York and driven up to the state university Eric attended to see his son. Upon arriving, he'd been shocked to discover that Eric had been placed in a mental hospital. Apparently, someone had seen him wandering around campus in the middle of the night, ranting and raving, and had contacted the authorities. He was suffering from schizophrenia, the doctors had said, and the school counselor had recommended that Steven withdraw his son from school and take him home for medical treatment.

Eric had struggled since high school. He was a native-born American citizen and had been raised on Long Island, but he had been the only ethnic Asian in his school. Perhaps inspired by his success-driven parents—one of whom was absent more than present due to business pursuits—he felt driven to impress by proving himself better than everyone else at just about everything. Keeping up wasn't enough. In school, he had to get the best grades. Among his peers, he had to be the most popular. And he had to outdo his friends in every area. When they drove fast, Eric had to drive faster. When they drank or did drugs, he drank or did, double. Before long, he had lost his stability and his sense of self, and his problems had become clinical. Some periods were worse than others, but it certainly didn't help that his father was rarely present.

"Every family has its problems," Helen had assured her husband. "That's why we need the love of God."

Steven had appreciated her words of support, as well as her piety. But, inside, he knew that he had never lost his business focus for the sake of his family. He hadn't been there for Eric when he'd needed him most.

All these things flashed through Steven's mind as he listened to Pastor Won talk about Father School. One was opening in Beijing, Pastor Won told them, with an enrollment fee of 5,000 *yuán*—about $600. It was the perfect opportunity for the fathers to take a step forward.

"Beijing is very far away," Steven objected, "and the cost will add up." Yet he knew that the distance wasn't the real issue. Things were going so well for him in Shenzhen with pastors Won and Cho, and he had just begun to rebuild his client base. He didn't want any interruptions. Nor did he want the added expense. Why, he questioned, did he have to pay to be a good Christian? After all, he'd been active in the church; he'd done his job. He was already serving the Lord. Did he have to surrender himself entirely?

"It's not so far," said Won, "just a few hours' flight. And it's only a four-day commitment—two evenings a week for two weeks." He had already promised to send a couple of members from his congregation, he revealed. Would anyone volunteer?

Steven looked around him. None of the men raised his hand. When he turned back to Pastor Won, he saw that his face had dropped; he was disappointed.

Steven couldn't bear to let his pastor down. He and his wife had given so much of themselves to foster Steven's spiritual life and had come to mean a great deal to him. Now, Steven was a senior member of the church, as well as a teacher. He had to set an example for the others.

Four days, he thought. *How big a deal can it be?* He remembered the Lord's call to Isaiah—*"Whom shall I send? And who will go for us?"*—and Isaiah's response: *"Here am I. Send me!"* (Isaiah 6:8).

"Okay, I'll do it," he agreed. "I'll go."

***

"Submit to one another out of reverence for Christ....
Each one of you also must love his wife as he loves himself."
—Ephesians 5:21, 33

When Steven arrived in Beijing, he joined seventy or eighty other men—all ethnic Koreans—in a big Chinese church. They had come from throughout the municipal area, Steven found out, recruited by pastors and graduates of Father School.

From the first moment Steven walked in, he somehow knew that Father School was perfect for him. It just felt right. Each daily session started at five in the evening and lasted about six hours, concluding around eleven or eleven thirty. The first day focused on the theme of "The Father's Influence." The men began by singing gospel songs together. Then, they broke into smaller groups of seven or eight, each led by a Father School graduate, and discussed the influence of their own fathers and their experiences with them.

One by one, each man was asked to share about the relationship he'd had with his father growing up. The men opened up to one another, and before long, there wasn't a dry eye in the room. Some of the men had loved their fathers; others had hated them; still others claimed that they hadn't had any feelings at all. Some men couldn't find it in their hearts to forgive their fathers; others sought forgiveness for themselves. Whatever their stories, the men supported each other, identifying with situations similar to theirs and sympathizing with those whose experiences had been more difficult.

Steven shared that he had hardly known his father—the family had never spent time together, and, when Steven was only six, his father had left him and his mother to live with another woman. Six years had passed before his return. When his father had died, Steven told the group, there hadn't been many happy times to remember; there'd been no tales of fatherly support or pride. He wept as he spoke, and the other men wept with him. Many of them had grown up in the midst of hard times, too, and the common denominator of their stories was a life filled with loss and pain.

At the end of the session, the men all wrote letters to their fathers. Steven, like the other men whose fathers had passed, wrote to his father as if he were still alive.

"To my father in heaven," Steven began. "Even though I didn't really know you, I still miss you. I wish you had lived long enough to see everything I've done." The letter was full of questions: "Why did you leave us? What did you do when you were gone?" There were so many things Steven didn't know. But his letter also contained a heartfelt apology: "I'm sorry, Father, that I didn't love you better."

Next, the men read their letters aloud to each other. Again, the room was full of tearful memories and revelations. When Steven read his letter, he felt relieved, as if a weight had been lifted from his shoulders. He was so glad that he had agreed to come to Father School. All the men exchanged tearful embraces before the session dismissed. They were brothers, they realized, joined by their stories of confession and forgiveness.

The second day focused on "The Man as Father." During the small-group meetings, when the men were asked to consider how they were similar to or different from their own fathers, Steven fully felt his shame. While he hadn't utterly abandoned his children, as his father had done to him, he wondered if he were really so different. On the rare occasions when he'd been in New York, he had devoted almost every waking hour to making money and spent most of his time away from the house. Even when he'd been there, in many cases, he'd been less than completely present. And then, he'd left Helen and the children all alone to establish his business in China.

Something else Steven finally realized was that he had never allowed himself to express his love. He'd thought that doing so would be a sign of weakness. Women showed their love, not men—not even fathers.

Steven was forced to ask himself some hard questions. Which had he loved better, his family—Helen and their three children—or his work? Whose company had he preferred, theirs or that of his partners, clients, and coworkers? Where had he actually invested his time and energy? To which had he given his all? And how honest had he been with them, and with himself, while at home *or* away? How much had he really missed them?

Again, the men wrote letters, this time to their children. They were asked to list twenty reasons why they loved them. Steven started out just fine, but by reason #12, he was having trouble coming up with any more. Eventually, he was able to complete the list, but in doing so, he saw that he should have valued his children more when they had been together. And he should have told them that he loved them.

Before the men left for the day, they discussed the same thing that Pastor Won had told Steven in Shenzhen—how the Lord, their Father, had blessed them all, and how they now had the responsibility to pass their blessings down to their children.

"Use Numbers 6:24–26," the group leader told them. "Put your hands on their heads and tell them, as the Lord told Moses to tell Aaron and his sons how to bless the Israelites, '*The LORD bless you and keep you; the LORD make his face shine upon you and be gracious to you; the LORD turn his face toward you and give you peace.*'

"This is the duty of the father," he told them. "Do this every day while calling out the names of each of your children."

The third session, during the second week, focused on "The Father as Husband." As they had during previous sessions, the men shared their feelings and recounted their experiences, this time as they related to their wives. Again, Steven couldn't help but compare himself with his own father. He hadn't run away to live with another woman, Steven told the group, but neither had he been entirely faithful to Helen. Most of the other men could relate. Like Steven, many of them had lapsed in their marital vows and been unfaithful to their wives.

When it came time to list the reasons why he loved his wife and then write a letter to her, Steven told Helen how much he loved her—and had loved her—since the very first day, when they had met over Cokes and cookies in the produce store. He begged for her forgiveness and promised to try to be a better husband when he returned to the States. It wasn't too late, the leader had told them, and Steven believed him; he felt determined to improve his marriage.

Finally, each of the men was directed to set up a date with his wife. He was to take her wherever she wanted to go, at whatever time was best for her, without anyone else present. And then, while he was seated across from his wife at dinner, he was to read aloud his list of twenty reasons why he loved her. "I promise you," the leader told them, "this will touch your wives' hearts. And so many of the problems you have in your marriage will start to go away, so many of the wounds will be healed."

Steven couldn't complete this part of the process immediately, of course, but he promised himself and Helen that he would do so as soon as he returned to New York. In the meantime, the Father School mailed his letter to Helen so that she could read his words of love and commitment.

On the last day of Father School, the wives of the participating men were invited for a special ceremony celebrating the spiritual meaning of being a father and a husband. As part of the ceremony, the women were seated in a row of chairs; their husbands then knelt down before them with a bowl of water and a towel, removed their shoes and socks, and washed their feet—all the while offering words of love and appreciation, confessing transgressions, and begging for their forgiveness.

Afterward, the couples prayed together. This was the climactic moment of Father School—husbands touching not just the feet but also the hearts of their wives.

Steven was sorry that Helen and his children couldn't be there for the ceremony. But he was no less thankful that he'd come. Not for a moment did he regret flying to Beijing or taking the time to attend Father School, an experience that would serve him for years to come.

7

NEW ARRIVALS

2001

"See, I will bring them from the land of the north and gather them from the ends of the earth. Among them will be the blind and the lame, expectant mothers and women in labor; a great throng will return."
—Jeremiah 31:8

Back in Shenzhen after graduating from Father School, Steven joined pastors Won and Cho for several exciting new preaching missions and membership campaigns specifically geared toward the working class.

Hiring in the province's factories had always been a challenge for employers, and the workers had long suffered under terrible conditions. For ten years, from 1966 to 1976, the Cultural Revolution had turned the Chinese culture and economy upside down. The youth had been trained as a Communist Party cadre, and anything remotely resembling a capitalist enterprise had been torn apart. Trained professionals and those with academic degrees had been ostracized, humiliated, and even imprisoned in "re-education" camps. Doctors had been forced to clean hospital floors while unqualified nurses treated their patients. It took years for the country to recover.

Two decades later, in the 1980s and 1990s, factory business was booming, but the workforce was mostly composed of untrained, unskilled people. Millions of Chinese were looking for employment, but there were far fewer reliable, experienced workers.

The vast majority of those who were hired were between the ages of eighteen and twenty-three, in part because of employer distrust of the older workers who had come of age during the Cultural Revolution. "If they're over thirty, don't hire them," Steven had once told one of his factory managers, echoing the common practice among business owners.

Almost all of the factory workers were migrants who had left their families to obtain employment and returned home only once annually, for two weeks, during the Chinese New Year. They were paid meager wages—little more than room and board—and were packed into group apartments and dormitories. Men and women were housed separately, even those who were married, and children were allowed only if they were old enough to work. If a woman had a baby, she had to quit.

These young, exploited workers, pastors Won and Cho recognized, would be open to preaching, and so, with the help of several church members who owned factories, they launched a factory mission. Once a month, thirty or forty parishioners would accompany doctors, nurses, and even barbers to the factories, where they offered free medical checkups, treatment, medicine, and haircuts. Working in teams, they would spend three to four hours serving the laborers, at the same time teaching them about the gospel and leading them in song and prayer. Knowing that Steven was involved—recognizing him as a reputable businessman whom they had worked with and trusted—the factory owners, some of them Christians themselves, were more than willing to trade the lost man-hours for the benefit of having steadier workers. Profit was their guiding principle, and as long as the activities didn't negatively affect production, they didn't particularly care one way or the other about the preaching.

Another of pastors Won and Cho's outreach missions targeted Shenzhen City residents with disabilities, who received little government assistance.

Pastor Cho saw an opportunity for both preaching and service. Under the protective banner of the Korean Culture Association, church staff members visited those with disabilities in their homes and sometimes took them to the city park for group picnics.

Eventually, the local newspapers got hold of the story and published this challenge: "Why do we Chinese ignore these people while foreigners are taking care of them?" It was good publicity for the "Korean Culture Association." Moreover, because the beneficiaries were Chinese citizens, and because the service didn't involve any overtly religious activities, it didn't draw the wrong kind of attention.

A constant goal of pastors Won and Cho was to increase the size of their congregation. They knew that over 10,000 ethnic Koreans lived nearby and that South Korea was about 25 percent Christian. So, they figured there were at least 2,500 Christians among the local ethnic Koreans. Yet, on any given Sunday, the three local churches counted a combined attendance of only 300. Had all the others given up worshipping communally? Where were they?

Steven helped pastors Won and Cho brainstorm ways of rooting out and attracting the "missing" Korean Christians. Pastor Won suggested they consider taking a chance and publicizing their services. The exposure could backfire and attract the government's attention, he admitted, but if they could spread the gospel by bringing in more Christian Koreans, he thought it might be worth the risk.

The following week, he placed an ad in the local paper. "Christian church," stated the promotion. "All Koreans welcome. No Chinese." No other Korean church had ever advertised itself; if anything, the goal was to avoid notice.

At least we'll beat out the competition, Steven thought. *I just hope it doesn't lead to any trouble.*

Sure enough, the exclusive appeal sparked a response, and the pews began to fill with Koreans. Among the new parishioners was a group Steven had never seen before—poor-looking strangers in ragged clothes who seemed quieter, shyer, and less open to conversation than the others.

Ever since the division of Korea in 1945, the north had practiced an isolationist program that had severely hampered its potential for economic growth. The success of its economy had depended partly on China but even more so on trade agreements with its primary military defender and closest ally—the Soviet Union. In the 1970s, North Korea's economy had started slowing down, and its reliance on a technologically outdated industrial base had left the country with a huge debt that it would never be able to pay off. In the 1980s, when the Soviet Union collapsed, these difficulties turned critical. Soviet support was cut in 1991, with exports to North Korea reduced by 90 percent. A North Korean energy crisis exacerbated the situation, as power output in the early 1990s decreased by half.

In an effort to boost agricultural yields from sparse arable land, largely infertile soil, and a harsh climate, the North Korean government established short-term land-use policies that almost guaranteed long-term disaster. Farmland was overcultivated through dated techniques that wasted energy. An electric-driven irrigation system helped raise the per-capita energy use to more than double that of neighboring China's, and chemical fertilizers, especially petroleum-based urea and ammonium sulfate, were contaminating the soil.

In spite of, or because of, the government's efforts, agricultural production in North Korea plummeted over the next decade. Soil nutrients declined by almost 80 percent, and by the mid-1990s—devastated by a flood that displaced more than five million people, destroyed 330,000 hectares of agricultural land, and led to the loss of almost two million tons of grain. The country found itself in the midst of a national famine.

In 1997, UNICEF reported that 80,000 North Korean children were in imminent peril of dying from disease or starvation; another 800,000—38 percent—suffered from chronic malnutrition. Over half of all North Koreans—more than twelve million people—were severely malnourished.

Estimates of the number of deaths from the famine ranged from two million to more than three million. As much as 15 percent of the population—in some provinces, more than 20 percent—died of hunger and famine-related disease. The country was starving.

The North Korean government's response to the famine conditions was inequitable and woefully inadequate. Instead of taking care of the entire populace, they divided the citizens into a hereditary political class structure, comprising three tiers, or *seongbun*: the "loyal," or "core," class; the "wavering" class; and the "hostile" class. Each *seongbun* was split further into fifty-one categories, and every citizen was required to register. A person's class determined his or her access to education, employment, housing, and federal assistance, including food. Residents of the provinces hardest hit by the famine were often relegated to the "hostile" class and received little, if anything, from the national food-rationing system, which, even at its peak, served less than 10 percent of the population. Desperate for food and unable to find employment, many North Koreans turned to theft, and famine-related crime was rampant.

At the same time, repression by the government had never been more severe. Public beatings and executions became everyday spectacles. Promoting Christianity—or any religion at all—was declared a crime against the state, and possession of any religious publications, including Bibles, was punishable by death. In 1991 alone, 400 Christians were reported to have been executed for their religious beliefs.

Few of those citizens accused of such "political" crimes were actually even arrested. More often, they were simply arrested, brought to an interrogation facility, and tortured until they "confessed." Then, they were taken away to *kwan-li-so*—sprawling prison colonies covering up to 400 square miles and run by the national security police.

When a North Korean was arrested, not only was he or she punished, but also, as stated in a 1972 edict from "Great Leader" Kim Il-sung, "Factionalists or enemies of class, whoever they are, their seed must be eliminated through three generations." Under the principle of *yeon-jwa-je*—guilt by association—parents, spouses, children, and even grandchildren of accused criminals were also imprisoned.

In the prison camps, which held anywhere from 5,000 to 50,000 people divided into separate "villages," families were forced to subsist on starvation rations in subhuman conditions. A typical daily ration was three servings of a few spoonfuls of cornmeal dissolved in water. To survive, prisoners would eat anything—animal feed, grass, bark, insects—whatever they could find that was even remotely edible or nutritious.

Kwan-li-so prison cells, intended to house up to twenty people, were often packed with sixty or more. They were unheated, without bedding, and often windowless or buried underground. Toilet facilities were rare, and in some camps, prisoners were forced to carry their own feces to a disposal area.

Modeled after Stalinist gulags and incorporating features of Nazi concentration camps, the prison colonies came to be known as sites of human experimentation and mass execution. Entire families were forced into glass-windowed chambers and gassed while doctors looked on and took notes. Prisoners were subjected to deadly injections in the development of chemical weaponry.

Even if they were married, male and female prisoners were strictly prohibited from having sexual relations; any woman who became pregnant in violation of this policy was forced to have an abortion. Prisoners charged with major infractions, such as those who had been caught attempting to escape, were publicly executed by means of hanging, shooting, or dragging by car; afterward, other prisoners were sometimes forced to beat, stone, or mutilate the corpses. Upwards of 200,000 people were imprisoned in the *kwan-li-so*, most of them for the crime of having "betrayed the motherland and people."

Desperate to escape the hunger, poverty, and repression of their homeland, North Koreans began a mass exodus across national borders, usually along the 870 miles shared with China. The Yalu and Tumen rivers provided navigable crossings, especially in the winter, when they were at least partially frozen.

In the early days of the migration, most of the refugees were relatively healthy males, and China did not seem to view them as a major problem, nor did it try to stem the tide. Once the refugees had crossed the border, the ethnic Korean population composing half of China's northeastern Yanbian Prefecture in Jilin Province provided human camouflage.

In time, however—especially during periods when the North Korean border patrol relaxed its vigilance—the exodus increased. More and more, the refugees were predominantly undernourished women and children, eventually constituting more than 70 percent of those fleeing North Korea.

The Chinese government started to crack down in earnest, determined to stop the influx of foreigners with no money or marketable skills. Article 33 in the 1951 United Nations Convention Relating to the Status of Refugees stated that "[n]o Contracting State shall expel or return (*refouler*) a refugee in any manner whatsoever to the frontiers of territories where his life or freedom would be threatened on account of his race, religion, nationality, membership of a particular social group or political organization." Despite being a party to this convention, China, following a secret agreement it had reached with the North Korean government in 1961, classified those North Koreans who had crossed its border not as refugees but rather as illegal "economic migrants," subject to arrest, imprisonment, and repatriation.

Chinese employers were subject to fines of thirty thousand *yuán*—about $3,600—if they hired North Korean refugees, and private citizens risked being fined one thousand *yuán* for protecting border-crossers or providing them any assistance. China dispatched a special contingent of undercover officers, assisted by North Korean security agents, to hunt down refugees. Rewards were offered for tips and information leading to a refugee's arrest. In the cities, embassies and consulates where North Koreans sometimes sought asylum were closely guarded by police, who would go so far as to cross through the gates and drag out any refugees attempting to enter.

On the run from the authorities and fearful of the Korean-Chinese people around them, the North Korean refugees looked for ways to blend in. This proved quite difficult, however; they were shorter than the Chinese and looked physically different from them, as well as from those ethnic Koreans who had lived in China for some time. Moreover, they didn't know the language. Some women married Korean-Chinese—or if they had to, Chinese—men. These marriages were mainly brokered, and most of them were far from ideal, but at least those women who married voluntarily were able to escape starvation, prostitution, imprisonment, or repatriation.

Less fortunate were the great majority of North Korean female refugees who, at the hands of human traffickers, were sold and resold into forced marriages and the sex trade. Some women were abducted by local gangs, some were drugged and then kept prisoner, and others were lured into slavery by well-organized professionals. The going rate was about $500 each, depending on age, health, and attractiveness, with many women and young girls being sold either to prostitution rings or to men looking for servant-wives or just sex slaves. Most of the women spoke no Chinese and were especially vulnerable without the protection of a father, husband, or other male in their lives.

Some of the women resigned themselves to their fate, especially if it meant being well fed. Their biggest fear was being caught and repatriated to North Korea, where they faced certain imprisonment, with mortality rates averaging 30 percent, and probable torture. If a returned refugee was suspected of having been contacted by Westerners, South Koreans, or missionaries, she was automatically convicted of spying and sent to a prison colony for a sentence of up to twenty years. Few prisoners lasted that long or ever made it out. Knowing well the perils of repatriation, male and female refugees alike did anything they could to avoid being sent back.

By the end of the 1990s, when Steven first began noticing North Koreans in the south, reliable sources estimated the number of refugees in China to be in the hundreds of thousands. *Newsweek* International reported "an estimated 300,000 [North Korean] refugees scattered across northeast China" alone, a number later seconded by the U.S. House of Representatives' Committee on International Relations.

Steven had heard about the plight of the refugees, and he'd known of missionaries who had tried to help them, but he had always made a point of minding his own business. Like the factory owners with whom he dealt on a daily basis, his focus had been fixed exclusively on making money. Unless it affected his income, it didn't matter much to him; if it threatened to get in the way of his profits, he wanted nothing to do with it.

But Steven's perspective had begun to change, thanks to his experiences at Father School and his church involvement. He started to take notice of these poor-looking, quiet Koreans who sat in the back pews and avoided his gaze.

***

"If a man owns a hundred sheep, and one of them wanders away, will he not leave the ninety-nine on the hills and go to look for the one that wandered off? And if he finds it, I tell you the truth, he is happier about that one sheep than about the ninety-nine that did not wander off. In the same way your Father in heaven is not willing that any of these little ones should be lost."
—Matthew 18:12–14

At church one Sunday, Steven noticed two filthy, shabbily dressed strangers sitting in the corner. They looked scared. *How could they have gotten here?* Steven wondered. Shenzhen was closed off. *They must have come through the mountains or around the checkpoints, or else climbed over the walls.*

After the service, Steven approached them. "Welcome to our church," he said in Korean. "Why don't you stay and have something to eat?"

The two were hesitant. They looked at each other, as if wondering what to do. At last, they agreed to stay.

During lunch, Steven asked them where they had come from, but they didn't reply to his questions and were reluctant to talk to him at all. *That's okay*, he thought. *I'll let them have some space.* The three of them ate together in silence.

After a while, once the two men had filled their stomachs, one of them answered. They were from North Korea, he admitted. They had crossed the Tumen River a few months before and had slowly made their way south, a distance of 2,000 miles, sleeping under trees in the countryside and in side streets in the cities, begging for food and watching out for security police. They had hoped to find a way out of China, he said—maybe to Vietnam, or, if they could get there, to South Korea, where they would be given automatic citizenship and welcomed like brothers. They were hungry, he added, and didn't know where to go. When they had heard there was an underground Korean church in Shenzhen, they'd risked their lives getting into the city. Was there anything Steven could do?

Steven excused himself for a minute and went to speak with pastors Won and Cho, who told him there was no possibility of the church taking the men in. They were already under suspicion, and if they were caught sheltering refugees, they would be arrested, and the entire church would be shut down.

So, Steven stepped up and offered to take them in. He was an American, he reminded them—the only one in the church. Nothing would happen to a U.S. citizen; his embassy would protect him if anything went wrong. And he didn't own a factory anymore, so what did he have to lose? He would take the men out of the church and away from Shenzhen, to Chang'an. He'd let them stay with him at his place for a while. Maybe he could find them jobs at one of the local factories.

There was no border check leaving Shenzhen, only coming in, so Steven had no trouble smuggling the two refugees back to Chang'an. The next day, he introduced them to one of the factory managers he knew, saying they were Korean-Chinese migrant workers. The manager didn't ask any questions. For now, at least, the two men had jobs and a place to live. But Steven didn't know what to do next. The two men might be able to blend in with the Korean-Chinese at the factory, but he had no idea how to get them out of China.

Nothing had changed when, a few weeks later, Steven received a call from the pastor of his home church in New York. The pastor told him that a missionary in northern China had contacted him and asked for assistance in helping a young man, a refugee, from North Korea. Would it be possible for Steven to at least give him a call, his pastor asked?

When Steven spoke with the missionary, the man described what was happening up north. They were seeing more and more refugees every day, he told Steven, and the Chinese government had turned up the heat. There were security police agents searching everywhere, and North Korean agents, too. He had been sheltering a young man at his place, but it was too dangerous to keep him there any longer. He had heard that the situation was better in the southern provinces. If he put the man on a train and sent him down, he asked, would Steven be able to take him in?

Steven couldn't argue. Being so close to Hong Kong, the people of Guangdong hardly even watched Chinese TV and were largely unaware of the refugee problem. Instead, they tuned in to Hong Kong networks, more interested in keeping tabs on the world economy and U.S. culture than in current events in their own area, including the situation with the refugees. North Korea was a world away for them, and they were too busy making money to notice.

Steven already had two men at his place; he figured he could make room for one more. He agreed to welcome the missionary's charge and to put him up, at least until he'd found work and could stand on his own.

Steven met the young man at the train station and brought him to his apartment. Kim Tae-nam was in his mid-thirties. He had been drafted into the North Korean army and served twelve years, he told Steven—the usual obligation. Then, when his term was finished, he had gone back to his home-town in the southeast, not far from the South Korean border.

When he had arrived, he'd been shocked by the living conditions. People were literally dying in the streets, he reported. Men wandered about aimlessly, jobless and without hope. There were no children outside—none of the run-ning and playing he remembered from his youth. All the doors were shut; few shops remained open.

When Kim Tae-nam had walked into his house, he'd been greeted by his mother—only in her fifties, she had shrunken to almost nothing: a tiny, bent-over old crone about to die. She'd said she wanted to cook him a special meal to celebrate his homecoming. He'd followed her into the kitchen, where she'd presented him with a bowl of rough, scraggly greens.

"What's this?" he had asked.

"Our food," she'd replied. "It's all we have." There was no rice, no meat, no fish, no vegetables. To stay alive, she had made a thin soup from some weeds she'd picked in a field.

Because he had served in the army, the young man had been able to get a week's supply of rice. At least he and his mother could eat for a few days, he'd thought. And he had already been set up with a job at a nearby factory.

The factory, the man had been told, employed almost 400 workers. But when he had gotten there, he'd found it practically deserted. A few men worked lethargically; operations were almost at a standstill. Everyone had left to find affordable food. As was true in most of the country, factory wages were not being paid. They had been replaced by food rations, but even those were not enough to feed the workers themselves, let alone their families.

The man had realized that if he wanted to live, he'd have to go elsewhere. He hadn't wanted to leave his mother alone again, but she had insisted. There was no way he would have survived if he'd stayed. So, he had left the fac-tory and his town. He had heard a rumor that there was something going on further up north, near the Chinese border. But there, too, he had found that people were starving, and there was no work.

Next, the man had heard that there was food in China, on the other side of the Tumen River. So, he had crossed. He hadn't known anyone there, he told Steven, so he'd sought help in a Korean church. At least they spoke the same language. There, he had met the Korean missionary friend of Steven's pastor, who'd helped him travel south.

Over the next few months, dozens of other North Koreans appeared in Shenzhen—both men and women, one or two almost every week. Steven hadn't had any trouble with the men he had helped so far; he had been able to find them jobs in a factory, and no one had commented about their presence in his apartment. But he still had to exercise extreme caution.

Afraid that the Chinese security police might send spies to infiltrate the church, Steven vetted the stories of the arriving refugees as thoroughly as possible. First, he asked them to retell their tales again and again, checking for inconsistencies. Then, he had them write out a full account of their journey, and he would verify the details with one of the North Koreans sheltered in Chang'an.

Every story broke Steven's heart, but he was especially touched by the accounts of the female refugees. One woman, after being tricked by traffickers into thinking they would help her, had been bought and sold six times to six different men. All of them had abused her, and she had suffered repeated beatings. Her last owner locked her in a room in his fifth-floor apartment and sent his friends in, one after another, to rape her. When she tried to resist, they punched and kicked her until she was bloody and fell unconscious. The next day, the man warned her that if she left the house even once, he would turn her in to the police. Finally, she couldn't take it anymore, and she jumped from a window, hoping to kill herself. Somehow—by the grace of God, Steven thought—she fell onto a heap of garbage and survived. She was discovered by a Korean-Chinese couple, who brought her to safety. They got in touch with a missionary they knew, who had sent this woman to Steven.

Another woman had been bought by a farmer to work the land and have sex with his two sons. Another had been chained to a bed and forced to service a series of men who paid her captor.

When Steven listened to the women's stories, there was little he could do but weep. He knew he couldn't turn them away. He thought of his own wife and daughter, safe at home on Long Island. He had vowed at Father School to go back to the States more often and spend longer periods of time with them, but, since the refugees had started arriving, he hadn't been able to get away. At least now, he assured himself, he wasn't just focusing on his own pleasures; he was fulfilling a mission.

He thought of God's words in the Old Testament about the terrible hardships of the Hebrews in Egypt. *"I have heard them crying out because of their slave drivers,"* the Lord had told Moses, *"and I am concerned about their suffering"* (Exodus 3:7). Steven was filled with compassion for these battered souls who had arrived at his door in such dire need.

8

CHANG'AN

2002

*"By day the LORD went ahead of them in a pillar of cloud to guide them
on their way and by night in a pillar of fire to give them light, so that they
could travel by day or night."*
—Exodus 13:21

Before Steven realized it, he had a dozen North Korean refugees under his
care—more than he knew what to do with. He had rented a second apartment
near his own, and then a third, to give them a safe place to stay; but, as the
number of refugees he was sheltering increased, so did the danger. And as the
refugees migrated south through China and filtered into the Guangdong, the
government's attention followed them. Steven had heard of nearby factories
being visited by members of the national security police, and the local officers
were becoming more aggressive in their vigilance. They posted public notices
offering rewards for information leading to the arrest of illegal foreigners, and,

one week, they went door-to-door to check IDs. Taxi drivers were given a hot-line to call if they sighted any suspicious strangers.

Steven had managed to find employment for the original three men in his care, but now, factory owners in the area had become more suspicious and less accommodating. They figured that some of the workers whom Steven had brought to them must have been refugees, and even the Christian factory owners didn't want to risk getting in trouble. They hadn't minded taking on one or two Korean-Chinese as employees, but they weren't willing to risk their livelihoods—and, quite possibly, their lives—by adding any more to their payroll.

Neither did many of the newcomers want to venture outside the apartment. Most of them stayed hidden in the safe house all day, afraid that if they left, they would be arrested and sent to a Chinese prison or, worse, repatriated to North Korea. Steven supplied them with cookware and brought them groceries and other provisions. On Sundays, he would go to church in Shenzhen, take notes from Pastor Won's sermons, and then preach the same message to the refugees in Chang'an. Sometimes, a church friend would ride back home with him and help lead the group in song and worship. All in all, it was a better life than the refugees had known in North Korea, but they lived in constant fear. What they needed was a way out of China.

Steven was aware that he couldn't hide the refugees forever, but he couldn't come up with an alternate solution. An entire year went by, and still he had yet to arrive at a satisfactory solution, even though the situation grew increasingly tense and risky with each passing day. He heard about one refugee who had made it safely to Seoul, but when he wrote to ask what route he had taken, the man demanded over thirty thousand *yuán*—about $4,000—for the information, plus another $4,000 for each refugee he arranged to help.

Too much, Steven thought. *I can't afford that.* But at least he was beginning to get a sense of the cost of the project—it wouldn't be cheap. He had been paying out of his own pocket to shelter the refugees. If the mission was going to progress—if he was going to succeed in getting them out of the country—he would need assistance. He spoke to his friends at the church in Shenzhen and also wrote to his church in New York, organizing fund-raisers during his trips to the U.S. For the first time, Americans were hearing about the plight of the North Koreans, and some wanted to help. The Shenzhen church agreed to cover the monthly rent for the safe houses, and some of Steven's supporters in New York committed to sponsoring individual refugees. Steven had the idea to set up a matching fund: for every dollar given, he would contribute one of his own.

Steven speaks at a rally in Washington, D.C., during a U.S. fund-raising trip.

Over time, using a combination of resources, he was able to establish a sustainable foundation. Now, he was ready to make something happen. Remembering the German industrialist who had saved over a thousand Jews during the Holocaust, Steven named the operation Schindler's Mission.

For the next stage, he turned to his most trusted adviser, Pastor Won. Steven knew of at least several refugees who had escaped China. He asked Won how they'd done it. Where had they gone? He had heard that there was a route through Vietnam. Did Pastor Won know anyone there?

As it happened, Pastor Won managed to find someone—another minister who was part of a larger group of Korean missionaries. "It's not a total solution," he told Steven, "but it could be a first step. The most important thing is to get the refugees out of China." Pastor Won gave him the minister's name and phone number. "Give him a call," Won told him. "Maybe he'll be able to help."

When Steven contacted the minister, the man suggested meeting to discuss the details in person. So, Steven obtained a visa, flew to Vietnam, and visited the minister at his Korean church there. The minister introduced him to one of the church elders, Khang Young-Won, who then introduced him to his driver's brother, who worked as a local Vietnamese guide.

This young man said that if Steven could transport the refugees west, closer to China's southern border with Vietnam, he would take them across to safety. It was a fifteen-hour train ride from Guangzhou, he said, and then another three-hour trip by bus. From the border, he would escort them to Ho Chi Minh City, in Vietnam, where they would stay for one to two weeks. From there, the refugees' expenses would be picked up by the South Korean government via agents from its version of the CIA. Another guide would then take charge and arrange their travel to Cambodia, where the Korean embassy would provide them with temporary passes that would see them through a flight to Bangkok, Thailand, and then, finally, to their destination: South Korea. The entire trip, from Steven's shelter in Chang'an to their arrival in Seoul, would take four to six months.

It was a long route, Steven thought, and the expenses would add up if he wanted to help more than just a few people. Yet the cost per person—$600, plus transportation and expenses—was only a fraction of what he had been previously quoted in China and Korea. He could manage it. All that mattered was the refugees arriving safely in South Korea. He had found his underground railroad.

The young guide traveled to China only on certain days, so Steven found out when he was available and made the necessary arrangements. There were spies all along the route, the guide had warned him; they needed to maintain the strictest secrecy to avoid detection. In order to monitor the refugees' progress after leaving Chang'an, Steven designated a separate phone number to take their calls and scheduled periodic check-ins at various stops as they made their way across Guangdong Province. He always informed the guide how many refugees to expect, what they looked like, and how they were dressed.

When a group arrived at the station, the guide wouldn't approach them right away. First, he would watch from a distance, for two or three hours, to make sure there was no danger. Only when he was convinced that they weren't being watched or followed would he emerge to meet them. Then, he would escort them to the border.

The plan worked. Steven had wanted to do a trial run with just two refugees, but when the guide told him that transporting a group of four or more would reduce the price per person from $600 to $450, Steven, ever the shrewd businessman, took him up on the offer.

The first group was made up of three women and one young man. Steven dressed them in clothes that wouldn't draw too much attention, gave them several hundred *yuán* to cover their expenses, and then, with hugs and prayers, sent them on their way. Their check-ins all went according to schedule, and when Steven didn't hear from them again, he hoped that the rest of their journey had proceeded smoothly, ending with a safe arrival in South Korea.

More than fifteen weeks passed before Steven heard from the guide in Vietnam. The first set of refugees had made it through just fine, he said; everything had gone according to plan. Their connections in Vietnam, Cambodia, and Thailand had held firm, and the refugees were all settled in Seoul. Steven breathed a huge sigh of relief—and then started preparing the next group for travel. Schindler's Mission was in business.

Steven's underground railroad ran smoothly for more than a year. By the spring of 2003, he had sent more than twenty refugees to safety. When he discovered that the cost per person would drop even further if he increased the number of refugees he received from the north and sent them along with a shorter turnaround, he started more actively seeking others in need of assistance. He became known among North Koreans as someone who could be trusted, and refugees arrived from all over China seeking protection at his shelter and help making their escape.

Steven would hear about refugees from a variety of sources. One of those who had made it to the south had four relatives still hiding out near the North

Korean border. An old friend from Father School knew of a stranded woman with a child. A church in Yanji was harboring a young girl. There was no shortage of refugees in need.

When the weather got warmer, Steven traveled to China's northern provinces and extended his contacts with missionaries and safe-house providers. In almost every city he visited, he found at least one or two North Koreans hiding out or on the run. By September, almost a dozen groups of four had traversed the escape route without mishap and made it safely to freedom.

9

FRIDAY, SEPTEMBER 26, 2003

Shenzhen

"Blessed are you when people insult you, persecute you and falsely say all kinds of evil against you because of me. Rejoice and be glad, because great is your reward in heaven, for in the same way they persecuted the prophets who were before you."
—Matthew 5:11–12

After a long yet routine week toward the end of September, Steven faced a busy Friday. At ten that morning, after telling his workers he would be out the rest of the day, he left the office for the nearby shelter. He was about to send the largest group ever—nine refugees, three men and six women—along the escape route. They would begin the long journey to Vietnam the following evening, and Steven planned to meet them for a morning prayer service before attending an afternoon dedication of a new education center at a nearby Korean church, at which he was to sing with the choir.

The morning traffic had begun to die down, so he made it to the shelter in good time. As he approached, he saw the regular day guard, standing out on the main road; for some reason, he wasn't walking his usual beat along the narrow path winding up to the building. Steven told himself to act normal and greet the guard on his way in. When Steven waved to him, however, the guard turned and looked the other way, down the street.

Steven noticed four men and one woman milling around the apartment entrance. None of them looked familiar. *Maybe they're new*, Steven thought. Many businesspeople rented apartments in the building; they were always moving in and out.

Hurrying along the narrow walkway, Steven saw a Chinese man dressed in a short-sleeved shirt, shorts, and sandals stop in front of another apartment. Then, on his way upstairs to the fourth story, he became aware that the Chinese man was following him up the steps. Behind him were two of the men and the woman from the group that had been standing outside. *They're probably going to another apartment*, Steven thought. But he was getting nervous. When he passed the second floor and continued up to the third, they were still following him. He felt sure something was wrong.

There was nowhere to go but up, so Steven kept climbing. On the fourth floor, he heard footsteps behind him—the man in shorts had caught up to him. Steven held his breath. But the man didn't stop; instead, he passed on to the next level.

No one lives up there, Steven thought. *I wonder where he's going.* Reaching the door of his apartment, Steven pulled out his keys, fitted one into the slot, and turned the knob.

Suddenly, the man in shorts turned around and raced down the stairs, while the men and woman below rushed up toward him. The man grabbed Steven and yanked his arms behind him. When the others reached him, one of the men showed Steven his ID card. "Military Border Police," Steven read—the guards of the Chinese-Korean border.

"Open the door," the man told him. His partner pointed a gun at Steven's face. When Steven turned the knob again, both men rushed in, guns first, shouting in Korean, "Freeze!" Steven could hear shouts and cries from inside.

In a moment, a dozen plainclothesmen and uniformed officers stormed up the stairs and into the apartment, guns out, pulling Steven with them. They rounded up the nine North Koreans and pushed them against the living-room wall. Bibles and hymnbooks dropped to the floor as the refugees were arrested, cuffed, and dragged downstairs, out to the street, and into waiting unmarked cars.

One plainclothesman pushed Steven into a chair in the center of the room and showed him a warrant to search the apartment. "I'm Deputy Officer Choi Chung-Ryong," he said. "Give me your passport."

"I'm an American," Steven protested. "I want to contact the American embassy. I want to call my office, my wife."

Ignoring his requests, the officer grabbed Steven's passport and strode into the other room.

For the next two hours, a dozen policemen searched the apartment, tearing the upholstery from furniture and rifling through Steven's papers.

Deputy Officer Choi, whose nickname, Steven later learned, was "Dragon" Choi, stood two feet in front of Steven and fired one question after another. "Where did you just come from?" he barked. "Who has been helping you?" "Are there any others?" "Where were the refugees going next?"

He interrogated him about the North Koreans, the church, Steven's business—all the places Steven had been, all the people he'd contacted, and all things he'd been doing. Somehow, Choi knew the whole story—everything.

It turned out that Choi and his partner had been trailing the latest group of refugees for over a week, all the way from the church that had sheltered them near the North Korean border. Police had been watching Steven's safe house—and Steven—since the refugees had arrived. Every movement, from their arrival at the train station to their transport to the apartment, had been recorded.

Choi informed Steven that two of the others involved had already been arrested and were in custody. Both were Korean-Christian women—one of them, a pastor's wife, had purchased the train tickets; the other had arranged for a van to take the refugees from the church to the train station.

Steven was terrified. He had heard multiple accounts of interrogations by Chinese officers and had seen some of those who had suffered through them. The son of one of the women he'd helped—a teenage boy—had crossed the Tumen River and stolen some vegetables from a local farm, having gone days without eating and having no money with which to purchase food. He'd been caught, and the local police had beaten him bloody and handcuffed him to a chair for three days, entering his cell only to shake him conscious and beat him again. By the time they were done with the boy, he had confessed to his theft—along with a host of other crimes he'd never committed—and had been sentenced to fifteen years. Even then, his punishment wouldn't be complete; he would be turned over to North Korean authorities to face further torture and imprisonment—and probable execution.

"I was so afraid," Steven recalled years later. "So I started to pray. 'What should I do, God? What should I do?'—this is how I was calling out to Him. And, somehow, Bible verses started coming into my head; I could actually hear them. *Do not fear,*' I heard, '*for I am with you; do not be dismayed, for I am your God.*' It was like God was talking right to me, speaking to me from Scripture. *'I will strengthen you and help you; I will uphold you with my righteous right hand.*' These were His words." (See Isaiah 41:10.)

When Steven heard these verses, his thoughts started to shift. *Why is this happening to me?* he asked himself. As if he were on the verge of death, his life began flashing before his eyes. He relieved the realizations he'd experienced in Father School regarding the kind of husband he had been, the kind of father—selfish and singly focused on financial success. *I've been living for myself,* he saw, *for my pleasure. I haven't been true to my family, myself, or my God.*

There's nothing I can do, God, he cried silently. *Nothing I can do on my own. I have nothing—nothing to lose. I'm a sinner. Do with me as You please.*

Suddenly, a great peace came over him. He felt totally helpless and, for the first time, totally surrendered—not to this officer who peppered him with questions but to his Lord God, in front of whom he sat, already convicted.

"Then I heard the voice again," Steven remembered, "very strong, very powerful. It was speaking from Mark 13:11 this time. *'Whenever you are arrested and brought to trial,*' it said, '*do not worry beforehand about what to say. Just say whatever is given you at the time, for it is not you speaking, but the Holy*

Spirit.' It was telling me not to be afraid, to tell whatever I felt—to speak out. 'I am the one who will give you the words to say,' God was telling me. 'It will be Me speaking, not you.'

"That calmed me, and I answered all of the officer's questions, telling him practically the whole truth—everything except the actual routes and the names of the people who had helped me. I described how I had successfully guided over thirty refugees to South Korea through China; how I had sheltered them, and led them along the trail, and helped dozens of others to escape North Korea."

Choi was shocked. Based on previous experience, he had expected Steven to deny everything and reveal nothing. Yet, here Steven sat, giving a full confession. Choi could hardly believe his ears. If what Steven had told him was true, he informed him—if he had helped as many North Koreans as he'd said he had—he would be sentenced to over twelve years of hard labor in a Chinese prison, American or not.

For some reason, however, Choi was conflicted; it seemed he wasn't sure exactly what to think. He had been sent by his government, by his country, to hunt Steven—to track him down, arrest him, and turn him over for punishment. That was his job, and he'd done it many times before. But Steven seemed different somehow. He was a man of principle, Choi could tell—a good person, not a hardened criminal. Choi was afraid for Steven's safety, he told him. He feared what would happen to him in the *laogai*. And he felt that he should try to do something to help.

Steven's confession had been recorded; it couldn't be changed. But Choi would see what he could do. He confiscated the Bibles, just as another half dozen policemen came through the door with another warrant—to search the building that housed Steven's office and residence. They took him out to a van to transport him there.

When the van arrived at the duplex, Choi escorted him up to his rooms without cuffs or shackles. He had given Steven strict orders not to say a word to anyone, and so Steven's employees had no idea what was going on.

Upstairs, the men searched everything, confiscating Steven's camera and laptop computer. In one dresser drawer, among his belongings, they found several stacks of money—paper bills in large denominations.

"What's this?" Choi asked.

"Payment for goods," Steven told him. "Here in China, I have to pay cash for everything. No one is willing to accept my checks or credit cards, not even my friends or office workers.

"Here," Choi said. "Take two thousand *yuán*. Hold on to it."

"Why?" Steven asked.

"You're going to need it in prison," Choi advised him.

"In prison I'll need money?" Steven wondered why this man was giving him the cash and telling him all this—helping him out. "What about the other nine people?" he asked. "Maybe I should take it for them."

"No," Choi replied. "That's it. Don't worry about the others."

Steven was taken to the Guangdong Province Coastal Military Headquarters in Guangzhou, where he joined the nine North Korean refugees in a ten-by-twenty-foot cell. When the police threw him inside, the others all crowded around him, crying and holding on to each other. He tried to reassure them, but he was almost as scared as they were. He had no idea what would happen.

Mug shot of Steven Kim

Guards banged on the iron door with batons and screamed at them in Chinese to break up the group. Reluctantly, the refugees released their holds on one another, but there really was no room for them to separate. A few sat against the wall, whimpering; one woman seated in the corner nodded off intermittently, always jerking back awake with a cry. All of them feared for their lives.

One of the three men in the group was a fifty-year-old who'd worked at a power plant in North Korea. He was a political refugee, and he knew that if he were repatriated, he would immediately be tortured and then executed.

Another refugee had converted to Christianity. The North Koreans were even less tolerant of religion than the Chinese, Steven knew. If the man were turned over, he would spend the next fifteen years in a prison camp—if he lived that long. Steven consoled him and whispered that he shouldn't tell the authorities about his faith.

"But I'm a Christian now," the man said. "I can't lie." Together, he and Steven prayed.

Steven felt an odd mixture of emotions: peace, fear, regret, and deep concern for these people whom he had tried to help. He knew their futures were bleak; if they survived the Chinese labor camp, they would be returned to North Korea, to be beaten and tortured, imprisoned, and maybe executed. He wished there was something he could do. Meanwhile, within himself, he was still wracked with guilt over his past misdeeds.

Because the refugees had come across China's northern border, and the officers who had arrested them had come from the north, as well, it was back to the north that they would be taken—Steven included. And he knew that didn't bode well. The judicial system was a little more lenient in the southern provinces; even with the recent crackdowns, the refugee issue wasn't as big a deal there, and the judges were likelier to deliver a more clement sentence. Up north, cases involving illegal refugees were tried almost daily—they were routine. Sentences were preset, and the prisons were ready.

Steven wished he could contact his Chinese office manager. She would be able to get in touch with Helen and inform the American consulate. But there was no possibility of making any phone calls. Once a prisoner was taken into Chinese custody, he or she had no rights at all—not for the minimum two months mandated for sentencing, even if you were an American citizen. Steven would simply disappear. No one would know where he was or what had happened.

When Steven didn't show up for work the next day, his secretary, Wendy, did call Helen and let her know he was missing. Helen then called the consulate and told them he was gone. They informed her that, for the moment, they wouldn't be able to locate him or obtain any information about what had happened. He was buried deep in the system, hidden in the dark labyrinth of Chinese bureaucracy.

Before they could locate him at the Guangzhou headquarters, Steven and the others were bound in cuffs and shackles and herded onto a northbound train.

10

YANJI DETENTION CENTER

2003

"Because I have sinned against him, I will bear the LORD's wrath, until he pleads my case and establishes my right. He will bring me out into the light; I will see his righteousness."
—Micah 7:9

At 11 a.m., after an arduous journey of thirty-six hours, the train whistle indicated their approach to another station. Steven caught a glimpse of the sign above the depot: *Changchun.* The guards prodded at the North Koreans with their rifles and motioned for them to stand.

It was a relief for the prisoners to leave the train, but no sooner had they disembarked than they were herded onto a waiting bus with barred windows. There they sat for the next eight hours, almost dead with exhaustion, the Koreans still chained in pairs, as the bus rattled further north, closer to the border.

When the bus pulled up to the gate, the door folded open, and a guard stepped in and pointed at Steven. "Get up!" he shouted in Chinese. All the refugees rose from their seats. "No!" he yelled again. "Just him."

Steven staggered out of the bus into the chill night air. Before he could even glance back, he heard the door creak closed and the bus chug up the road, carrying away his North Korean brothers and sisters. It was Monday, September 29, he remembered. He would never see them again.

The guard escorted Steven through the heavy gate and into the concrete-walled prison. A sign above the front entrance announced in Chinese, "Yanji Detention Center." At a reception desk, he was freed from his cuffs and shackles and told to strip. He stood there naked and watched another man take his clothes and leave.

At another desk, Steven was processed and issued his prison rations: two T-shirts, a set of long underwear, two pairs of underpants, a pair of slippers, a blanket, a towel, a toothbrush, and a tube of toothpaste. Later, he learned that the money from his office had been deposited into an account, from which 440 *yuán* had already been deducted to pay for his provisions.

After processing, Steven was taken to cell number 18—a sixteen-by-ten-foot space with a wood-planked floor and a sink and open toilet in one corner. Pausing in the doorway a moment, he counted seventeen men inside—thirteen on one side, four on the other. The thirteen were smaller in stature, and they huddled together like frightened animals, crouching on their haunches or lying in the fetal position. The other four stood in relaxed poses—large, fearsome men with tattoos of warriors, flowers, and tribal symbols running up and down their frames.

Steven tried to look calm, but he was terrified, practically trembling as he held his provisions close to his chest. All he knew of prison was what he had seen in Hollywood movies—violence and murder, gang rapes and abuse. From the appearance of the figures before him, he wouldn't have to wait very long to experience these horrors firsthand. *Lord have mercy*, he silently mouthed.

The guard shoved Steven into the cell, and the iron door clanged shut behind him.

One of the four—a massive, huge-muscled man with elaborate designs covering his arms, legs, and torso, including a giant dragon writhing up and across his back—took a step forward and faced Steven head-on. "I'm in charge here," he announced in Korean. He looked a bit older than the others, probably somewhere in his forties. "You're over there." He pointed to a space near the other three, who stood, watching.

Uh-oh, Steven thought. *They're all murderers. I'm being set up.* He held his belongings even tighter, as if they would protect him.

But then, the cell leader gave him a slight nod. "You'll be fine," he said. "You're with us."

The man's name was Kim Kwang-ho. He was the cell leader, as well as the boss of an entire branch of the Korean-Chinese mob, leading not only this small prison gang but also an entire criminal organization on the outside. He was in prison for murder.

On behalf of the authorities, the cell guard had given Kwang-ho advance notice of Steven's arrival. Steven was an American, the guard had told him, and he didn't want any trouble. If anything happened, the prison authorities would hold the guard responsible—and he, in turn, would hold Kwang-ho him responsible.

In addition to this warning, and just as important, Steven had money. So, Kwang-ho treated him well, even kindly. He gave him an extra blanket, a worn towel, and a pair of slippers with rubber soles. "They'll help keep your feet dry," he said. "That way, your skin won't rot." Steven was charged another seventy-five *yuán* for the slippers, about nine dollars, but he was thankful to have them.

He was so tired and hungry, he could barely see straight. He sank to the floor, desperate for sleep. Before drifting off, Steven prayed—more fervently than ever before. "Dear Lord," he whispered, "please help me submit to Your will. Please reveal to me why I'm in this place, and tell me how to serve You. Amen."

***

"While Joseph was there in the prison, the LORD was with him; he showed him kindness and granted him favor in the eyes of the prison warden."
—Genesis 39:20–21

Steven awoke early the next morning, just after dawn. To his astonishment, on the floor near his head was a Korean Bible. He couldn't believe it, nor did he understand; other than his clothes and essential provisions, he hadn't been allowed to bring anything in—no books, and certainly not a Bible.

Oh, my God—thank You! he thought. *You haven't forgotten me!*

He looked around to see who might have given him such a gift. Everyone else seemed to be sleeping, but then, a boy next to him opened his eyes and whispered in Korean, "Are you a missionary? I saw you praying last night. I thought you might need a Bible." It had belonged to a prisoner who'd been executed, he said; it had been given to the man as his last wish.

"My name is Kim Kyong-il," the boy told him. "I'm from North Korea. I taught Bible classes in Beijing and was arrested for aiding refugees, like you. I was watching when you came in."

"Thank you," Steven said. "By the time I finish it, I'll almost be ready to go home."

Kyong-il smiled sadly. "Are you kidding?" he asked. "You'll have to read it *ten* times, and even then you might not be released."

Steven was shocked.

"The man you replaced in the cell," the boy said, "Ko Hui-ju, was a South Korean businessman who had come to China to collect some money that was owed to him. When his debtor didn't pay, Hui-ju had had him kidnapped and held for ransom. He was here for a year and a half before being transferred for the rest of his term."

"Is that normal?" Steven asked.

"People are usually kept here for at least six or seven months," said Kyong-il. "Then, they may be transferred or released, but some are held much longer. Chong-man, a Korean-Chinese from Changbei, is here on the same charge as we are—helping refugees. He's been here for six months. I've been in for sixteen. I was sentenced to four years, but I knew I was better off staying in a Chinese prison than going back to North Korea. So, I confessed to more crimes, ones I didn't commit, to extend my prison stay. They added eight years to my sentence. At least I won't be going back to North Korea anytime soon."

One of the policemen at Steven's arrest—not Choi—had told him that since he was an American citizen, he would probably be held for only two or three months. Now, Steven realized that his stay could last quite a bit longer. As he'd understood it, a detainee had to be charged within thirty-seven days of capture; otherwise, he or she had to be released. After charges were filed, the prosecution office had two months to confirm the charges and then another two months to investigate. After that, the case would go to trial—all told, six or seven months, tops. Clearly, Steven had been mistaken.

Then, something clicked. Steven was already in his mid-fifties, but he had read the Bible only once, and not seriously. In Shenzhen, he had participated in pastors Won and Cho's regular Bible study group, but they had progressed only halfway through the Good Book. Now, he felt like he was hearing God's voice again, this time speaking through this young man. To go home, Steven realized, he would have to read the Bible—not just once but ten times!

Kyong-il and Steven looked into each other's eyes. Then, without saying a word, they clasped hands and knelt together in silent prayer.

***

"In the desert prepare the way for the LORD;
make straight in the wilderness a highway for our God."
—Isaiah 40:3

Steven had been assigned a prime sleeping spot on the "first-class" side of the small cell. He saw immediately how helpful Officer Choi had been when he was apprehended. With the two thousand *yuán* Choi had advised him to bring, Steven was assured a standard of treatment denied the average prisoner.

His status as an American helped, since the prison authorities wanted to steer clear of any government scrutiny or criticism, but money, Steven knew from all his years in business, was the international language, spoken as fluently by his imposing, tattooed cell leader as it had been by the furniture merchandisers in New York.

Each cell was divided into three classes, which were recognized by the guards but determined and enforced by the prisoners themselves. The first class comprised the few who had money, connections, or just sheer physical power. They were in charge and enjoyed extra provisions, choice sleeping spots on the floor, and better food—in bigger quantities. There was a prison restaurant for the guards and other workers, complete with a menu; the prisoners were forbidden to go there, but it was possible to bribe the guards and pay inflated prices for a meal delivery. The prisoners weren't allowed to carry their own money, and so the funds were kept in accounts from which their expenses were deducted.

The first-class prisoners hired other inmates to do their cleaning and chores. In Steven's cell, the four gang members chose two of the others to serve them, including Kyong-il. He and another prisoner-servant formed the middle class. They weren't paid, but they could earn a degree of protection, as well as slightly better conditions and treatment, by doing the first-class prisoners' bidding.

Below them were all the rest. With eighteen men in such a small cell, there wasn't enough room for everyone to lie down at once, so the third-class prisoners had to sleep in three-hour shifts. Even then, they had to huddle together on their sides, front to back. When awake, they stood or crouched in place. At mealtime, they were given only a piece of grainy corn bread and a bowl of salty seaweed broth. And they were treated harshly by the guards and other prisoners. If one of them showed even the slightest hesitation at the command of a guard or a first-class prisoner, he was beaten without mercy.

Steven could see the look of fear in the third-class prisoners' eyes as they cowered before the cell leader and his men. There was a constant tension in the cell, but it was controlled by Kwang-ho, who, with a mere arch of his eyebrow, could dispatch one of his gang members to beat a prisoner into submission.

Steven could also see the third-class men, weak with hunger, watching him when he received his meals of soup and a bowl of rice from the kitchen. The first time, he mixed the rice with the soup and ate only half of it, thinking he would save the rest for the others. But when he tried to share the remaining portion with the other prisoners, Kwang-ho grabbed the bowl, took a few spoonfuls himself, and gave the leftovers to his men. Steven realized that he had no choice in the matter. So, seeing that eating and sleeping were his keys to survival in prison, he resigned himself to eating his food without sharing.

Altogether, there were thirty-three prison cells in Yanji, each cell holding between seventeen and nineteen prisoners. There were also two female cells, separate from the men's, for a total of over six hundred detainees awaiting trial.

At the end of his first week at Yanji, Steven saw what became of North Korean prisoners who protested their conditions or tried to make their cases known to the rest of the world. One prisoner from the next cell had applied for political asylum and asked to speak with representatives from the United Nations and Amnesty International. His original sentence was four years, but after his appeal, his sentence had suddenly been reduced to time served, and he'd been scheduled to be sent back to North Korea.

"I don't want to go! I don't want to go!" the man had shouted in fear. The next night, four government agents had come and cuffed the man's hands behind his back, covered his head with a black hood, and then beaten him savagely with truncheons, right in his cell, in front of the other prisoners. Then, they had taken him away. None of the inmates ever saw or heard from him again, but the message had been delivered.

Ten days after Steven's arrival, the entire prisoner population was moved to a new detention facility adjoining the old one. It had between seventy and eighty cells, most of them housing thirty prisoners each, the exception being six "luxury" cells with a capacity of twelve. These six cells featured irons beds and pallets, and the going rate was a thousand *yuán* a month—about $130—plus an extra charge for a bed. This amount was double the salary of most factory workers, and few prisoners could pay it. But, for those who could, the cells were more spacious, and a bed would save a man's body from the pain of sleeping on a cold, hard floor every night.

Steven, wealthy by prison standards, immediately gave the guards a full month's payment for both a "luxury" cell and a bed. After two weeks of tortured nights in the old building, he was finally able to sleep through till morning.

Although the living conditions had improved, the basic detention-house rules remained the same. There was no work detail, but the prisoners were locked in their cells 24/7. During the day, they had to sit up straight on the bare wood floors and keep totally silent and still. The only exception was during the ten-minute breaks, occurring every fifty minutes. Otherwise, they were to remain motionless. If they stretched, they were beaten. If they stood up, they were beaten. If they spoke, they were beaten more.

After a few days, Steven's ankles had become bruised and swollen; they hurt so much, he thought they were broken. He asked a guard for medical attention, but all he got was a jab in the ribs with a baton and a brusque order to shut up and sit back down.

Early in the morning was Steven's only time of peace. Every day, he would arise two hours before the 6 a.m. wake-up call to pray, meditate, and read the Bible. It was not forbidden for him to pray; he just couldn't talk to the other prisoners or include them in his worship.

There weren't any cell gangs in the new facility, and Steven didn't feel threatened by the other prisoners. As had been the case in his former cell, the prisoners—even the cell leaders—didn't want any trouble from the prison authorities; the authorities didn't want trouble from the Chinese government; and the government didn't want trouble from the United States. As a result, Steven was comparatively safe. And he had the firm conviction that he was the righteous opponent fighting a fierce spiritual battle.

Through his daily Bible reading, Steven's spiritual understanding began to deepen. He completed his first Bible read-through within nineteen days. Then, remembering Pastor Won's instructions about quiet time, he slowed himself down, pausing for reflection and prayer. In the next eleven months, he read the Bible ten more times, feeling that he'd penetrated the text more deeply with each reading.

Living in such tight quarters, the other prisoners couldn't help but notice that Steven practiced constant prayer, Bible reading, and meditation. Some of them, Christians and unbelievers alike, were attracted to his piety. He slowly made a few friends in his cell, and he began preaching to them in secret.

Many people were in great need, Steven knew, but especially among these inmates. Outside of the long period when they had to sit up straight, starting before eight in the morning and extending past four in the afternoon, they didn't know what to do with themselves, unless they were eating or sleeping. Sadder yet, spiritually speaking, they were totally lost. All that most of them did was complain about their fate and persist in proclaiming their innocence. For them, prison was a living hell.

Ever since those hours immediately following his arrest—when Steven had confessed his worldly crimes to Officer Choi and his moral and spiritual crimes to the Lord—he had known how guilty he was. It was ironic, he could see, that it had taken his arrest for the "crime" of aiding his North Korean brothers and sisters for him to indict himself of his real crimes against his family and God—failing to be a good husband, a good father, a good Christian. His judge for these offenses was not the Chinese government or any police authority but his Lord and Savior. And he was determined to change his ways.

Prison will be my "wilderness" school, Steven decided with heartfelt conviction. *Moses thought he could lead the Israelites out of Egypt under his own power, and I thought I could rescue the North Koreans. But there's nothing I can do on my own. Here, I'll be trained by the Holy Spirit.*

Every hour, Steven promised—every minute—would be an opportunity for confession and repentance. Already, for him, prison was not the hell the other prisoners were experiencing but the perfect place to cleanse himself of guilt. He felt sure that it was God's grace that had placed him in the midst of such harsh conditions, and he wasn't about to waste this opportunity. Hopefully, it wouldn't last for forty years.

***

"And now these three remain: faith, hope and love.
But the greatest of these is love."
—1 Corinthians 13:13

After searching through practically the whole Chinese prison system, the American consul finally tracked Steven down in the detention house. The consol informed Helen that Steven was alive, but she wasn't allowed to see him. Steven wasn't even permitted to seek legal counsel. By Chinese law, during the initial investigation period, only the government investigator could meet with a prisoner; no outside visitors were allowed. Once a month, the consul was allowed to check on Steven's physical condition and make sure he wasn't being abused, but, even then, the consul was accompanied by two or three security officers. He and Steven were never left alone or permitted to discuss his case.

Fortunately, Officer Choi didn't forget his commitment, and, for the first two months of Steven's incarceration, Choi was his only outside friend. During Choi's official "investigations," he visited Steven regularly to ensure his safety and well-being. He supplemented Steven's account with funds from Steven's office when the balance was low, and he even smuggled in Bibles, writing materials, and warm clothes. Steven was grateful for the provisions. It was nearing winter, and the prison had no hot water and practically no heat. The damp stone walls did little to hold in whatever meager warmth the prisoners' bodies generated.

During Choi's visits, he would express to Steven his misgivings about having landed him in prison. In turn, Steven started preaching to Choi, telling him about St. Paul the Apostle, who had vigorously persecuted Christians during the first century C.E. Paul, named Saul at the time, experienced a dramatic conversion after a vision of the resurrected Jesus on the road to Damascus. Paul, Steven told Choi, went on to preach the Word of Christ and to write nearly half of the New Testament.

Steven started reading the Bible to his fellow prisoners. Groups of more than two prisoners were forbidden, and silence was enforced all day long, but, whenever he could, in the mornings and evenings, Steven read Scripture to anyone who would listen. Somehow, he had to find a way to reach them and get them to listen.

To gain acceptance by the other prisoners, Steven began volunteering to sweep and mop the cell floor—two tasks nobody else wanted to do. In order to really win them over, he knew he would have to extend himself beyond just doing some chores; he would have to earn their respect, maybe even their affection. And to do that, he'd have to develop feelings for them himself. He would have to look into his heart and find love.

Steven prayed for assistance, asking God to teach him how to open his heart. He searched through the Bible and found 1 Corinthians 13:1–3:

If I speak in the tongues of men and of angels, but have not love, I am only a resounding gong or a clanging cymbal. If I have the gift of prophecy and can fathom all mysteries and all knowledge, and if I have a faith that can move mountains, but have not love, I am nothing. If I give all I possess to the poor and surrender my body to the flames, but have not love, I gain nothing.

But what does love mean? Steven asked himself. *I thought I loved my wife and family, but then I treated them poorly. If I was like that to them, how should I treat these prisoners, whom I don't even know?*

He read on in 1 Corinthians 13:

Love is patient, love is kind. It does not envy, it does not boast, it is not proud. It is not rude, it is not self-seeking, it is not easily angered, it keeps no record of wrongs. Love does not delight in evil but rejoices with the truth. It always protects, always trusts, always hopes, always perseveres.

(1 Corinthians 13:4–7)

"Thank You, Lord," Steven prayed aloud. *I've always tried to be good to other people,* he thought, *but I have to do more than that. It's not just my behavior I have to change but how I actually feel.*

Steven did his best to translate his resolution into action. He wasn't sure if he was actually doing anything differently, but when he looked at the other prisoners, even those who spit, swore, threatened others, or engaged in violence, he tried to view them with compassion, with love. He knew how much he looked down on some of their bad habits, but he tried to be patient with them and not to consider himself as their superior. When good fortune befell them, he rejoiced; when they suffered, he suffered, too, following the apostle Paul's exhortation in Romans 12:15.

Steven couldn't tell for certain if his new outlook was having any effect. Still, inside himself, he knew that he felt better. Before long, having witnessed his piety, his humility, his ability to care for others, and his willingness to come to their assistance, the other men started treating him differently. And they began calling him "Pastor Kim."

Steven's cell mates were a diverse lot. Chang Kui-Min, age forty, was a Chinese banker accused of embezzling his investors' funds. He was a tangle of contradictions, and Steven couldn't quite figure him out. He spit everywhere and seemed never to clean himself, but at night, he wrote poetry.

Chang Kon-Mun, age fifty-six, had been a county mayor who had gotten into conflict with others in authority and was accused of abusing his power of office. Steven could see that Kon-Mun still thought he was better than the other prisoners; he was used to being in power and, even in prison, didn't see others as his equals. But Steven knew that, inside, Kon-Mun was suffering just like the others.

Young-Bum was a young man—*Six months younger than my son Eric,* Steven remarked to himself. His mother was in South Korea, his father in Russia. He had been living with his aunt and, finding little by way of amusement, had started hanging out with a rough crowd. One night, a friend of his had gotten in trouble with a security guard, and Young-Bum had jumped into the fight. He had been arrested, and when the police had searched him, they had found a knife. He had been in Yanji for five months without any official charges filed against him. *How sad,* Steven thought, *and all for associating with the wrong people.*

Another man, Joseph Brown, was a Nigerian who, like Steven, had originally come to China for business, shipping manufactured goods to Brazil from his office in Shenzhen. To make up for a cancelled order, Joseph told Steven, he had bought a plane ticket for one of his client's friends who was leaving China. When the friend was arrested for smuggling drugs, Joseph was implicated. He had been arrested, beaten, and tortured at the station house, then sentenced to death on the charge of drug trafficking. And all he'd wanted to do, Steven reflected, was to repay his client.

Another cell mate, Stephen Zhou, had recently been appointed president in charge of Asian operations for a billion-dollar pharmaceutical manufacturer, a Fortune 500 Company, based in New Jersey. Steven recognized the man's story as typical of many he had heard in China. When Stephen had arrived in China, he had found many things amiss and had fired several upper-level Chinese managers. In retribution, the brother of a former company officer had contacted friends in the regional police department and had Stephen charged with accepting kickbacks. Stephen was arrested and sentenced to twelve years. Six months after his arrival in Yanji, he'd been stabbed and blinded in his left eye, and he wore a rough-hewn patch over it.

Steven's most aged cell mate was Moon Gil-Joong, a sixty-one-year-old Buddhist who slept in the next bed. Moon had a small bracelet of black stone prayer beads, which he wore around his right wrist at all times. He would chant using the beads almost constantly, rolling them around in his fingers while mouthing a Buddhist mantra.

Moon admired Steven's devotion to prayer and would sometimes join him in the early morning to pray and sing. They followed the hymns printed in the back of one of the Bibles Choi had brought in.

After a few weeks of worshipping together, Steven asked Moon, "Which do you believe in, Buddha or Jesus Christ?"

"Both," Moon replied. "I need Buddha to help me and Jesus to help me—everything to keep my faith."

"You have found your Buddha," Steven told him. "But the Lord is jealous. Jesus is saying, 'If you put down your Buddha, I will help you.'"

Moon's eyes opened wide. "Why?" he asked. "Why would God be jealous?"

"'First you worship with Me,' He is saying," Steven replied, "'and then you worship another.' You have to choose."

Moon thought it over for a few days. Then, he told Steven, "Okay. I'll try Christ."

"Great," Steven said, "but you'll have to pray only to Him. Otherwise, He'll be jealous. 'Our God is a jealous God,'" he recited from the hymn. "You can pray to only one."

"Okay," Moon said. Yet, over the next few days, Steven saw him still chanting over his beads.

"What's this?" Steven asked. "Do you truly accept Jesus Christ as your Savior, or are you still holding on to your old Buddhist beliefs?"

"I guess I am," Moon replied. "They're not as easy to give up as I thought they'd be. I've been practicing Buddhism for twenty-two years. I've built two temples. I can't just suddenly throw that all away."

"But God wants you to," Steven insisted.

Moon didn't agree. "I guess we can't worship together after all," he finally said. From then on, Steven would complete his morning service, and then, when he was done, Moon would have his Buddhist service, also with song and prayer.

11

PRAYERS AND MEDITATIONS

Visits and Journal Entries

With a pencil and paper that Choi had brought him, Steven began to keep a daily journal. The guards didn't seem to mind him writing, he found, as long as they thought he had no way of smuggling his writings out of prison. He would deal with that later. For now, he was satisfied with being able to sit down and write once a day.

Sunday, October 19

Devote yourselves to prayer, being watchful and thankful.

(Colossians 4:2)

"I got up at 4:00 a.m. today, my usual time, to pray and read the Bible and catch up with my daily prayer. It's too early for the others. Everybody was still sleeping, and the cell was quiet, almost peaceful. I want to try to give my first hour to God every day. I've been praying, but I've been lazy about it. I haven't been giving myself 100 percent. I have to seek forgiveness, and to do that I need some discipline—to be regular and get up early. If I stick to waking up early, reading the Bible, and singing God's praise in song—well, I don't know that I'll hear His voice, but I do believe that He'll listen to mine; that, if I start my day like this every day, He'll hear my prayer.

"This morning, I asked Him for forgiveness and strength. I prayed for my North Korean brothers and sisters who were arrested with me. I prayed that the Lord may give them His grace and peace while they are in prison, that He may grant them the strength to hold on to their faith. I prayed for them not to be discouraged or lose hope. I asked for forgiveness for my mistakes. The refugees are having so much trouble because of me. I promised that I will have more trust in Him and follow His will.

"'Lord who controls my life,' I prayed, 'I dedicate my life to You and to help all the North Koreans and refugees. I offer You whatever talent I have, Lord. Please use me as You will. Please give me the determination, Lord, to obey Your words every day, throughout my life. Amen.'"

***

After prayer, Steven read from the book of Matthew, starting with chapter 15. *The blind leading the blind—what a perfect image of our modern society*, he thought. *Instead of turning to our churches for leadership and worshipping the Lord, we put athletes and entertainers on pedestals and worship them instead.*

While reading, he realized that even though he had believed in God for many years, he hadn't actually felt His Word directly, very close to him. Now, only one month into his time at Yanji, Steven had read through the entire New Testament once already, and he was reading it again, and more intensely. He noticed for the first time that even though Jesus performed many miracles, His disciples still lacked faith in Him. When He walked across water to reach them, they thought He must be a ghost. When He multiplied the loaves of bread, they still feared hunger. Only Simon professed his faith, and Jesus called him Peter, because he was like a rock, and upon Peter He built His church.

Monday, October 20

Set your minds on things above, not on earthly things.   (Colossians 3:2)

"Today, I woke up early, at 3:30 a.m., from a weird dream. In the dream, I was driving a van, but, suddenly, it was stolen from me, and I had to chase after it on a bike. I wonder what it means.

"I was thinking about that, and then I started worrying about my family and all the other things going on outside, especially my business. Today was the first day of the Canton Fair, China's oldest and largest trade exposition, which I always attend. I'm sure all the buyers are there, placing orders for merchandise to bring to America, and I felt like I should be there, too, offering different product lines for them to sample. I had the idea to display items not just from the factories I usually dealt with but also from a range of different factories, especially the ones nearby.

"Then, I stopped and saw what I was doing. Here I am in prison, but I'm still so attached to my material ways—so conditioned by them. I have to stop that kind of thinking. I still haven't given up my greed for fortune. I'm not as interested in fame, but I still keep scheming about new ways to make money. It's getting in the way of my prayers and spiritual life.

"So I got up and splashed water on my face to help me put aside my worries. I resolved to try harder to put aside the things of this world and focus on the only things that are actually important in this life.

"I got on my knees and prayed. I was meditating on Psalm 6, a song of repentance:

> O LORD, do not rebuke me in your anger
>   or discipline me in your wrath.
>
>
> Be merciful to me, LORD, for I am faint;
>   O LORD, heal me, for my bones are in agony.

My soul is in anguish.
  How long, O LORD, how long?

Turn, O LORD, and deliver me;
  save me because of your unfailing love.

No one remembers you when he is dead.
  Who praises you from the grave?

I am worn out from groaning;
  all night long I flood my bed with weeping
  and drench my couch with tears.

My eyes grow weak with sorrow;
  they fail because of all my foes.

Away from me, all you who do evil,
  for the LORD has heard my weeping.

The LORD has heard my cry for mercy;
  the LORD accepts my prayer.

All my enemies will be ashamed and dismayed;
  they will turn back in sudden disgrace.

"In my meditation I started coming up with some new plans, not for my business but for others:

1. Through the Korean churches, keep Schindler's Mission going, and have an organized system to help North Korean refugees in China. I was accused of being a ringleader. Maybe I should really become one, make some connections, and build one main route.

2. Revise the old system and finances to unify operations and create different groups for maximum efficiency.

3. Form a mission program to help the youth in Yanbian—teenagers with single parents or broken families, as well as troubled kids and those in the correction centers.

4. Expand Korean churches in China. Include other people in the mission projects—like the Chinese, even though we don't speak their language. We should follow the example of David Brainerd, who spread the gospel to Native Americans even though he didn't speak their languages. When he was a teenager, he devoted himself to his mission and worked hard for nine years with full faith in the Lord, converting more than ten thousand people before he died at the age of twenty-eight. He can teach us that even though we don't speak Chinese, if we approach people bravely, with prayer and passion, we can get people to accept Jesus Christ as their Savior. If we want to accomplish our mission, we must have strong faith and a spiritual connection with God through prayer.

"I thank You, God, for giving me the opportunity to meet other Christians and know of their ministries. Thank You for giving me the Bible to read. Everything is from Your grace, and I thank You."

Sunday, October 26

Is not this the kind of fasting I have chosen: to loose the chains of injustice and untie the cords of the yoke, to set the oppressed free and break every yoke? Is it not to share your food with the hungry and to provide the poor wanderer with shelter—when you see the naked, to clothe him, and not to turn away from your own flesh and blood? Then your light will break forth like the dawn, and your healing will quickly appear; then your righteousness will go before you, and the glory of the LORD will be your rear guard.

(Isaiah 58:6–8)

"I've decided to fast on Sundays and started today. Everyone in the cell is surprised and thinks it's really strange. The usual practice here is to try to eat as much as you can. Food means survival. When I explained that I wanted to devote the day to God and not take anything for myself, they just looked at me. Actually, they were really happy, since it meant there would be more food for them.

"Choi Young-Sun asked me why I was fasting. 'If you fast, does anyone respect you more?' he asked.

"I told him that when I fast, I can focus better on my devotions. 'The power of my prayer is multiplied tenfold,' I explained. He looked like he understood, but it was hard to tell.

"Food is the most precious thing in prison, but I want to sacrifice something, offer God the most important thing I have. Really, I offer up my heart.

"Prayer of thanksgiving: Lord, thank You for bringing me here to Yanji Detention Center. If I had stayed in Guangdong, I would not have known all these many Koreans and Korean-Chinese who have lost their freedom.

"Thank You for helping me realize how lazy I have been, and for providing me with this Bible so I can meditate on Your Word every day.

"Thank You, Lord, for giving me this time of healing, for me to change my ways and not waste my life in material pursuits. Amen."

***

After two months had elapsed, Steven was allowed another visit from the American consul. He told Steven that everyone was worried about him and sent him their love. Steven wanted to tell the consul his whole story, but, as before, they were denied privacy and therefore could not speak freely. For the duration of the consul's visit, he and Steven were surrounded by officers, guards, and staff from the prosecutor's office. The consul agreed to deposit additional funds in Steven's prison account and promised to do everything he could to secure his release.

Finally, Steven was able to talk to Helen. Never in his life had he heard a more wonderful voice. She was fine, she assured him, and was taking care of everything in his absence. As soon as she'd heard what had happened, she had flown to China and taken over the office in Chang'an. She had gone through the paperwork, paid the bills, and collected payment on the open accounts. All of the money he'd had left—over $30,000 in cash—was accounted for.

Some of the office workers had not respected her, and she said she understood. After all, they had never met her before; they didn't know the extent of her business experience. But she'd had to fire several employees and hire replacements. "You wouldn't recognize the office staff anymore," she told him. "Only one remains whom you would know."

She was in control, she said; he had nothing to worry about. The Chinese factories had resumed their shipments to the U.S., and all was going smoothly. At first, his customers had been concerned about his arrest, but they'd soon realized that business would proceed as usual. One had even commented, "Wow, you're even better than Steven!" Almost all of their customers had stayed on. One Korean customer had severed ties, but all of their American clients remained steady; they expressed appreciation for the mission work Steven had been doing and pledged their loyalty to him and the business.

"I love you," Helen told Steven. "We all do. And we miss you very much. Make sure to take care of yourself; we'll be fine."

Steven could barely manage a reply. "I love you," he said in tears. And then they had to hang up.

Tuesday, December 2

> *As God's fellow workers we urge you not to receive God's grace in vain. For he says, "In the time of my favor I heard you, and in the day of salvation I helped you." I tell you, now is the time of God's favor, now is the day of salvation.* (2 Corinthians 6:1–2)

"My face and body hurt. There are six steel beds on each side of the room. Mine is along the wall next to the window, across from the door. I liked this spot when I first came, since, in October and November, the sunshine from the window kept me warm and the light made it easier to read. But now it's colder and the sun doesn't shine in the same direction. Last week, drops of moisture started beading up on the wall, and it gave me a wet chill. I woke up in the middle of the night in terrible pain, especially where I'd been facing the wall, on the left side of my face.

"I got up at four o'clock and drank some water, but I couldn't get rid of the pain. There's no comfortable way to lie down. When I sleep with my back to the wall, I get pain in my back. When my shoulder is close to the wall, it hurts, too. I can understand why some people hurt everywhere when the weather is bad.

"My stomach has been swelling and hurting. Helen told me that MetLife cancelled my life insurance due to my bad liver. Maybe this is my problem.

"I've offered my life to You, God—my business, my family, and my health. Let Your will be done.

"I was reading in Corinthians about God's grace. It's time is now here in Yanji. When I was in despair after my business went bankrupt, God showed me His grace and comforted me. He helped me overcome that hardship. Now that I'm here, there's nothing I can do but depend on His helping hand.

"It is amazing grace that I have God at all, even if I have no rights or anything to offer Him. He is always willing to give to anyone. Whoever is seeking will be saved. I will do my best work to lead those here closer to the Lord.

Wednesday, December 3

> Be very careful, then, how you live—not as unwise but as wise, making the most of every opportunity, because the days are evil.
>
> (Ephesians 5:15–16)

"Dear Lord, time flies like an arrow. Give me wisdom to manage and use time wisely in Your grace."

Thursday, December 4

If they have a change of heart in the land where they are held captive, and repent and plead with you in the land of their conquerors and say, "We have sinned, we have done wrong, we have acted wickedly"; and if they turn back to you with all their heart and soul in the land of their enemies who took them captive, and pray to you toward the land you gave their fathers, toward the city you have chosen and the temple I have built for your Name; then from heaven, your dwelling place, hear their prayer and their plea, and uphold their cause. (1 Kings 8:47–49)

"Monday night, the guards didn't go home but stayed overnight on standby. We all wondered what it was about. Yesterday morning, the door guard said, 'Four executions here today.' I wanted to pray for them. Even if, just before death, they repent and accept the gospel, they could be saved. God, have mercy on their souls. Accept them, comfort them, and bring them to You. Open the way for them to be forgiven.

"My face is swollen. Not a big deal, but yesterday my upper right lip started itching and getting warm, and this morning my feet swelled up. Maybe it's just lack of movement. God will not leave me to fall here.

"During the afternoon break I finished Bible study with Brother Choi Yong-Son. We studied, praised, and prayed while everyone else talked or slept. When we were done, the door guard told me that if I were Chinese and was seen sharing the gospel, I would spend the rest of my life in prison."

Even when I am old and gray, do not forsake me, O God, till I declare your power to the next generation, your might to all who are to come. (Psalm 71:18)

"I feel much better this morning. I was worried about the swelling in my face, lips, feet, and stomach, but now they all look normal. I have some appetite and feel better.

"My cell mate Chang-Hwa says he's about to go crazy with boredom. If I were more fluent in Chinese, I would share the gospel with him. We need a Chinese Bible.

"I received another book, which I've started reading—*Standing Together: Impacting Your Generation* by Howard Hendricks from the Dallas Theological Seminary and Promise Keepers. He writes about the prayers and example of the prophets Elijah and Elisha, and about passing on the mantle of Christian leadership to the next generation.

"Hendricks made me reconsider my motivations for helping the refugees. Was I doing it just for them? Or did I also want to inflate my own ego, to be someone 'important'?

"I realized that I don't pray enough. James, who we know as 'the brother of the Lord,' knelt in prayer so much that he was called 'Camel Knees' because of his calluses.

"Stuck in the book, I found a sheet of paper with the "ten commandments" that Rockefeller's mother gave him:

1. Honor God as your own father.

2. Honor your pastor next to your God.

3. Worship in your own church on the Lord's Day.

4. Put one-tenth of your earning in your right-side pocket, to be donated to the Lord.

5. No matter the circumstances, keep your promises.

6. Start each new morning with a joyful heart.

7. Each night when you go to bed, look back over your day.

8. Don't forget to greet God every morning when you rise.

9. Whatever you do, do it with thankfulness.

10. During church services, sit in the first row.

Friday, December 5

When anyone hears the message about the kingdom and does not under-stand it, the evil one comes and snatches away what was sown in his heart. This is the seed sown along the path. The one who received the seed that fell on rocky places is the man who hears the word and at once receives it with joy. But since he has no root, he lasts only a short time. When trouble or persecution comes because of the word, he quickly falls away. The one who received the seed that fell among the thorns is the man who hears the word, but the worries of this life and the deceitfulness of wealth choke it, making it unfruitful. But the one who received the seed that fell on good soil is the man who hears the word and understands it. He produces a crop, yielding a hundred, sixty or thirty times what was sown. (Matthew 13:19–23)

"I didn't feel well last night. Couldn't eat. God, You told me to leave all my worries to You, but I pray that I'll be able to carry out Your mission in the midst of my illness. You taught us to live for others, but many times I fail to live a life of love. I have a passion to teach the Word, but I lack wisdom. Lord, have mercy on me and pour down Your grace upon me. When I was reading from the book of Matthew with Brother Choi Yong-Son, I realized that I lack so many things. I pray that You will grant me the power of the Word and Holy Spirit and pour down Your mercy on this brother. Let his lukewarm heart be filled with lava to burn for Your Word. Please reign in Park Moon-Gil's heart so that he may understand Your power. He does not have faith toward You yet, but, Lord, please control his mind and heart so that he can become a man of God.

"Lord, I am embarrassed that I always go away from You, even when You have poured down Your unconditional grace upon me. I confess that I have lived my life only for myself and my desires, and I thank You, God, for leading me here so that I can be closer to You.

"Brother Son Yong-Wei came to talk to me after our sitting-still time. He's been here for fifteen months. He used to be a public security officer in Hwaryong City. He has been learning English from me for over a month now. Every day we talk in English about one theme. He's communicating better.

"He asked me, 'How can I be a good father?' He is thirty-seven, with a Japanese-Chinese wife, and he wants to be a better father to his ten-year-old son. He's a sincere and diligent man. He wakes up at 5:30 a.m., reads, and works out at night. I hesitated to answer him, since I'm not such a good father that I can tell him what to do, but then I thought about what I had learned in Father School. So, I gave him the following suggestions:

1. Restore the relationship with your father.

   Brother Son said his father is alive, but that he was not that great of a father. I asked him if he had ever in his life written his father a letter. He said no. I told him that in order to recover the relationship he should do so. "Write anything you want to say," I told him, "including any complaints. Try to reconcile. Your son will see how you and your father's relationship is restored, and then your son will do the same with you. You should speak to your father about the hurt that you've felt, so that you are able to forgive him and be forgiven. This will help your relationship become one of love and friendship."

2. Check your priorities.

   "Fathers are men," I said. "Men have their own lives. In what part of your life do you spent most of your time? Work, entertainment, alcohol, your social life?" Brother Son said that he is a workaholic. So, I told him to be free from work and try to spend more time with his family.

3. Tell your son that you love him.

   I told Brother Son to write down twenty reasons why he loved his son—why his son was beautiful to him. And to share that list with his son.

4. Think about the mission of father.

   Fathers want their children to have only the best. "I have God the Father," I told him. "Who do you have? As you suffer in jail, who do you have that you can trust and depend upon? God gives me power. When I am in difficult situations, He provides me with courage and help. The father must be a king of the family, a priest of the family. He must be both a teacher and a friend. He must be a warrior who fights for his family's survival, to keep his family together. Have you ever thought of these things as being a father's mission?" I asked.

5. The father must be steadfast in his spirituality.

"When your son is in trouble," I said to him, "who will he turn to? Who do you turn to? Lead your son to God, hand down your belief to him."

"Brother Son agreed with all these points, especially the ones about manhood and mission. He said he will practice them when he goes home.

"Lord, please remember Brother Son and lead him to be a great father. Thank You for these two months I've been with him and for our relationship. Please help me be more diligent and sincere."

Saturday, December 6

We, however, will not boast beyond proper limits, but will confine our boasting to the field God has assigned to us, a field that reaches even to you. (2 Corinthians 10:13)

"In 2 Corinthians, the Bible tells us that God has assigned us a 'field.' He has His plan. I'm here in Yanji to spread the gospel. It is not because my plan or my work; it is all in His hands. Yes, it is God who sent me here, to meet people and to minister to them. I give thanks to God for His works."

Sunday, December 7

I will rejoice in the LORD, I will be joyful in God my Savior. The Sovereign LORD is my strength; he makes my feet like the feet of a deer, he enables me to go on the heights. (Habakkuk 3:18–19)

"After this morning's prayer, I finished the Old Testament for the second time. Each verse has so much to say and is so important. No matter how many times I read the Bible, I don't think I'll understand it all.

"It took me twenty days, longer than I expected, but I was reading the commentary alongside the text. It's more important to fully understand the Word than to read it fast. It took more time but I learned more, too.

"One verse reminded me of the hymn 'The Lord Is in His Holy Temple':

The Lord is in His holy temple
Let all the earth keep silence before Him
Keep silence, keep silence
Keep silence before Him.

"Now I understand better about God, creation, the corruption of men, Abraham's faith, blessings, grace, promise, and sin and punishment. People are so foolish to repeat the same disobedience that led to sin and our cursed condition, even after learning about God's reign. Still, I understand. So many times I, too, was in the midst of God's blessing and love, but this sinful body turned away from Him. Still, God told me that if I remain with Him and keep Him with me, not only I but a thousand generations of my descendants will prosper. Thank You, Lord God. Please grant me more faith not to be weak. Amen."

Tuesday, December 9

This is what the LORD *says: "Your wound is incurable, your injury beyond healing. There is no one to plead your cause, no remedy for your sore, no healing for you."*   (Jeremiah 30:12–13)

"Yesterday morning the head of the detention center, Officer Cho, let us go outside for a little while. There was a foot of snow on the ground, so it was hard to walk in our slippers, but it was great to be outside for a few minutes.

"I'm having trouble with my nose. I went to the medical office, but the only 'doctor' there, taking care of hundreds of prisoners, is a veterinarian. He gave me an ointment, but it didn't help. He just told me not to touch it."

Wednesday, December 10

People will be lovers of themselves, lovers of money, boastful, proud, abusive, disobedient to their parents, ungrateful, unholy, without love, unforgiving, slanderous, without self-control, brutal, not lovers of the good, treacherous, rash, conceited, lovers of pleasure rather than lovers of God—having a form of godliness but denying its power. (2 Timothy 3:2–5)

"In my dreams last night God spoke to me about my sins. I'm not here because I violated China's law against helping refugees; God sent me here because of my disobedience and violation of His divine law. I thank Him for redirecting my life and reminding me of His blessings and grace throughout my life.

"God led me to the U.S. to live in the midst of the Word, but even when His blessings on my material life were overflowing, I was self-indulgent and driven by pleasure. Now he's taken everything from me, all because of my sins.

"In my morning prayers, without being conscious of what I was doing, I cried out, 'Lord, now I know. I'm nothing but a sinner.'

"I'm so thankful that God is helping me understand that in my pride, lust, and desires, I sinned against Him. I have to cleanse myself in the blood of His cross. I want to throw away my old self and be reborn. Help me, Holy Spirit; I am so weak. Please have mercy on me and forgive my sins. I promise to serve You with my whole heart.

"Yesterday, Officer Choi brought me some new clothes. He had to come in wearing two pairs of underpants and socks and three tank tops. He brought me a family picture, too. When I see him, I think of the apostle Paul. When Paul met Jesus, he was transformed from a persecutor to a follower. Choi told me that the police are now searching all over China to catch refugees, not just in the north; there's no place to hide.

"It's almost Christmas. Choi deposited four hundred *yuán* in my account. I want to buy cakes to send to the other prisoners and a few of the guards, but I'm not sure the guards will let me, even though I've been paying them off. I gave a pair of socks, a tank top, and a pair of underwear to Moon Gil-Joong. I feel very sorry for him; he has no family.

"Choi said that he's going to pass my case over to the prosecutor's office soon. Then, he won't be able to come see me more than once a month. A prosecutor will come instead. I hope my case will be done as soon as possible.

"Lord, I leave everything in Your hands. Thank You for Your grace."

Thursday, December 11

Therefore I will praise you, O LORD, among the nations; I will sing praises to your name. (2 Samuel 22:50)

"Last night, I had another dream, a wonderful one of grace. I rarely have any dreams that have to do with church. This one was just about a simple task—cleaning a room in Shenzhen. It wasn't very clear, but I remember the words 'for God's glory.' The words kept repeating, and I know they're true. Lord, please help me to remember these words. Whatever I do, I do for Your glory.

"I miss church, especially on Sundays. I never appreciated it as much as I do now. Worshipping in the temple of the Lord is such a great blessing. In Shenzhen, all of us in the choir would wear a gown. We'd enter the sanctuary at 10:40 a.m. and see everyone waiting in their seats. The pastor would be meditating as he got ready to lead us in prayer and give his sermon. I miss the whole congregation raising our voices together in song. Giving Him our thanks and praise. Passing along the peace of God. Our prayers for those in need. Accepting the Lord's Holy Communion.

"During the announcements at the end of the service, I would run and change into a kitchen apron to serve lunch. I miss the love and fellowship we shared when we looked into each other's eyes. All blessings.

"I wonder if the worshippers in Shenzhen today know how lucky and blessed they are—how they would feel if their freedom was snatched away.

"All brothers and sisters of churches around the world, I rejoice for your blessings. When will I be able to enjoy them again? I wait for the day, Lord, when I will be able to enter Your house of worship. Give me grace to wait patiently for that time to come again."

Friday, December 12

And I tell you that...on this rock I will build my church, and the gates of Hades will not overcome it. (Matthew 16:18)

"This is really the week of dreams. The other night, Moon Gil-Joong dreamt that he had built a church. Some monks he had trusted for twenty years came with cymbals to distract the worship, but Brother Moon told them to leave. He told them that he would get some people to force them out, but then he woke up.

"'Hallelujah!' I exclaimed when he told me. 'You are blessed to build a church in a dream.'

"A few weeks ago, he said to me, 'Pastor Kim, when you come to Korea, I'll build a church for you.' I think he fulfilled that in his dream."

12

ARTICLE 318

"Then Jeremiah said to King Zedekiah, 'What crime have I commit-
ted against you or your officials or this people, that you have put me in
prison?'"
—Jeremiah 37:18

A few weeks later, Steven's case was turned over to a prosecuting officer. He told Steven that he had been in contact with the consul, Steven's office, and Helen, and that he'd agreed to tell the court and write in his report that Steven had not been the ringleader of the refugee effort but only an assistant. That was crucial, Steven knew, since the leader of such an operation could be sentenced to death.

A date was set for Steven to appear in court. There wouldn't be a trial, he'd been told; this was just another stage in the process. To date, he hadn't actually been charged.

In court, Steven met the two women whom he'd heard had also been arrested, and who were also being held in Yanji. Their names were Lee Young-Ok and Lee Bok-Ja. Over a hundred people from their church congregation were in the courtroom, wailing and crying. Steven now had legal representation, but his attorney, a Korean-Chinese former prosecutor who had been appointed by a church friend of Steven's in Shenzhen, didn't seem to be of much help. "Don't worry," the attorney told Steven. "Your sentence will be a maximum of one year."

Steven also met with the American consul, Helen, and his sister, Hye-Kyung. They told him that Helen had been raising a storm of criticism in America. She had contacted congressmen, senators—anyone in a position to exert political pressure.

Representatives from the embassy had met with Chinese Foreign Ministry personnel, who had agreed to review Steven's case and do what they could to help out. Encouraged by his lawyer's assurances and the consul's report, Steven hoped for a light sentence—maybe time served and a few more months, less than a year altogether.

After three hours of waiting in the seats reserved for accused prisoners, Steven and the two women were told that their sentences would be handed down "later." They were then returned to the detention center.

The following week, Officer Choi came to visit. With him was a young, good-looking woman whom Steven had never seen before. She was a supervisor, Choi told him; she wanted to talk with him. Steven was hesitant, and when the woman stepped out for a minute, he told Choi, "I don't know. Things seem to be going well, and I don't want to mess them up."

"It's okay," Choi said. "Your case is almost ready for the sentencing stage; it's almost over."

Choi's been a friend, Steven reminded himself. So, he agreed.

When the woman returned, she was accompanied by a man with a camera and a microphone.

"What's this?" Steven asked.

"Don't worry," Choi replied, "She just wants to record what you say."

For the next half hour, Steven was interviewed by the woman about his case. When they were done, she left with Choi and the cameraman, and Steven didn't think any more about it.

A week later, however, Steven was brought to one of the prison's public areas, where there was a television. On the screen, on prime-time China Central TV, there was the woman, reporting on his case. "This is the man who led it all in southern China," the woman was saying. "This was the American ringleader, the one in charge."

It turned out that the reporter had been hired by the police to make Steven's case public. The government wanted to show the Chinese people, and the whole world, that they were cracking down on illegal refugee activity. They didn't want anyone helping the North Koreans, and they had to set an example. Steven was portrayed by the station as the worst kind of villain—a conspirator and an American spy who had organized a criminal network to undermine the People's Republic.

Facing the camera, the reporter read Article 318 of the Chinese criminal code covering Crimes of Obstructing the Administration of Public Order— specifically, Crimes Against Control of National Border (Frontier):

Whoever makes arrangements for another person to illegally cross a national border (frontier) shall be sentenced to fixed-term imprisonment of not less than two years but not more than seven years and shall also be fined; if he falls under any of the following categories, he shall be sentenced to fixed-term imprisonment of not less than seven years or life imprisonment, and shall also be fined or be sentenced to confiscation of property:

(1) being a ringleader of a group that makes arrangements for other persons to illegally cross the national border (frontier);

(2) repeatedly making arrangements for other persons to illegally cross the national border (frontier), or making arrangements for a large number of persons to do so;

(3) causing serious injury or death to the persons for whom he makes arrangements to illegally cross the national border (frontier);

(4) depriving or restricting personal freedom of the persons for whom he makes arrangements to illegally cross the national border (frontier);

(5) resisting inspection by means of violence or threat;

(6) the sum of illegal earnings being huge; or

(7) other especially serious circumstances being involved.

Whoever, in addition to the crime mentioned in the preceding paragraph, kills, injures, rapes, or abducts and sells the persons for whom he makes arrangements to illegally cross the national border (frontier) or commits other criminal acts against them or kills, injures or commits other criminal acts against the inspectors shall be punished in accordance with the provisions on combined punishment for several crimes.[1]

Steven's heart dropped. Now he knew he was really in trouble. "This is outrageous," he said aloud. "That law is supposed to stop exactly the criminals I was saving the refugees from—the human traffickers and victimizers! How can they accuse me with them?"

The American consul filed a protest with the station, demanding—he later told Steven—"How can you do this to an American citizen? How can you show his name and face and say he's a criminal—the ringleader of a criminal organization—when he's only a suspect? He's only been arrested, not even charged, let alone convicted."

But Steven knew that no judge would want to show leniency in a case that had been targeted by the government to receive such public attention. If anything, the courts would start ganging up against him. Sure enough, later that week, a judge from the provincial court came to see him. "Did you know that your government sold weapons to Taiwan?" the judge challenged him. "Chinese people don't like your country."

Steven was not necessarily surprised by the judge's comments, but they were certainly not what he wanted to hear.

As it turned out, "later," in regard to the reading of Steven's sentence, meant after several months. On June 25, he was again summoned before the

---

1. People's Republic of China, Criminal Law, Part II, Chap. VI, Sec. 3: Crimes Against Control of National Border (Frontier). Adopted July 1, 1979, by the National People's Congress, revised March 14, 1997, and promulgated by the President of the People's Republic of China, March 14, 1997. http://www.cecc.gov/pages/newLaws/criminalLawENG.php.

court. He wore a T-shirt, light green sweatpants, and slippers—the only footwear he was permitted—and a jacket given to him by one of his Bible students. Going out in public, he felt suddenly self-conscious. His hair had grown long, he thought, and his beard looked scraggly.

On the way out of the prison, he was again joined by Lee Young-Ok and Lee Bok-Ja, both of them dressed in prison orange.

The three of them were escorted across the prison compound and through the gate to a white van marked "Court Police." The women sat in front; Steven sat in the back with two armed policemen. No talking was allowed.

After a twenty-minute drive, they pulled up to the Middle Class Yanji City Court. Steven saw that the area in front of the courthouse was packed with hundreds of protesters, restrained by wooden barriers and monitored by police with shields and batons. The crowd looked to be made up almost entirely of Korean women, many of them from the church the two female prisoners attended. They were crying and calling out their names, and those near the van reached out their hands, as if to touch the prisoners within the stopped vehicle. While some of the policemen pushed the crowd back with their shields, others pulled Steven and the women out of the van and whisked them inside the courthouse.

One of Steven's cell mates at the detention house had told him that he was friends with the chief of the court police. Steven half expected one or more of the officers to greet him, but no one called his name. As the doors closed behind them, Steven could still hear the shouts from the crowd outside.

The courtroom was jam-packed. Steven saw Helen and his sister, with the American consul seated behind them. Officer Choi sat along the side. As Steven and his fellow defendants, flanked on both sides by four guards, were led to stand in the middle, facing the front, he felt that every eye in the room was on them. To one side was a row of attorneys; to the other, the prosecutor and two assistants. A court stenographer sat off to one side; there were no jurors in attendance. One minute later, everyone stood up as three black-robed judges entered the room and seated themselves on high-backed chairs facing the crowd, the chief judge in the center. Above their heads was the Chinese flag, red with five gold stars.

One of the judges delivered a brief opening statement in Korean, and then the defendants were asked to state their names, nationalities, and ages for the record. The prosecutor then read the charges, and Steven's lawyer was asked to state his case.

After a short break, during which the judges consulted with each other, Steven was called forward and directed to offer a final statement to the court. He delivered it just as he had practiced in the detention house, telling the judges that he wanted to apologize to the officials who had to do so much work to prosecute him.

The presiding judge asked him whether he regretted his actions.

All around him, Steven heard the wailing of women in the gallery. He was shaking, but he knew what he had to say. "If the same situation had happened to my son," he told the panel, "and my son asked me what he should do, I would tell him that he should do exactly the same thing I did."

Next, the two women were asked to step up and give their statements. Lee Young-Ok said through her tears that she was proud to be a Chinese citizen. She regretted having violated the law and begged for mercy and forgiveness from the court. Lee Bok-Ja spoke similarly, appealing to the court's sense of compassion.

"Very well, then," the judge replied. "We are ready to announce our verdict. In the case of the People's Republic of China against Steven Kim, the defendant is found guilty and sentenced to five years of hard labor."

13

AUGUST 27, 2004

Tiebe

"If you follow my decrees and are careful to obey my commands,...I will look on you with favor and make you fruitful and increase your numbers, and I will keep my covenant with you....But if you will not listen to me and carry out all these commands, and if you reject my decrees and abhor my laws and fail to carry out all my commands and so violate my covenant,...I myself will be hostile toward you and will afflict you for your sins seven times over....And you will be given into enemy hands."
—Leviticus 26:3, 9, 14–15, 24–25

To no one's surprise, Steven's appeal received little attention and was summarily denied. Chinese law since 1982 had mandated that all accused persons be tried and sentenced within sixty days of their arrest, but it hadn't taken long for Steven to learn that the reality was far different. The two-month window was rarely enforced and often ignored altogether; some prisoners, especially North Koreans, had been held for years without sentencing. One of his Korean cell mates had been in Yanji for five years without even being charged.

After eleven months in the detention center, Steven was ready for the next stage. His trial was over, his sentencing complete, and his appeals exhausted. Now, he was scheduled to be transferred from the detention center in Yanji to a more permanent facility—a work prison, a *laogai*.

Steven accepted his fate with calm resignation. Once the initial shock wore off, a strange composure came over him, much as it had after his arrest. He knew why he was being punished, after all. He had committed crimes against his family, against his wife, against his business associates, and, worst, against his God. It was time to pay for those. If it was God's will that he be imprisoned for his offenses, who was he to question that will?

Two days before Steven's scheduled transfer, Reverend Choi, one of four other pastors imprisoned in Yanji, invited Steven to his cell. Like Steven, Rev. Choi had been arrested and imprisoned for helping North Korean refugees. He had pleaded with the guard on duty to allow him and two of the other pastors to hold one last meeting with Steven.

Steven had lunch with the reverends Park and Choi. Afterward, they prayed together and read from the Bible, selecting a passage from the book of Acts.

> *On the Sabbath we went outside the city gate to the river, where we expected to find a place of prayer. We sat down and began to speak to the women who had gathered there. One of those listening was a woman named Lydia, a dealer in purple cloth from the city of Thyatira, who was a worshipper of God. The Lord opened her heart to respond to Paul's message. When she and the members of her household were baptized, she invited us to her home. "If you consider me a believer in the Lord," she said, "come and stay at my house."* (Acts 16:13–15)

In this story of conversion and service, Paul and Silas were bringing Christianity into the Macedonian region, to Philippi, for the first time. There was no church there, not even a synagogue. But when Lydia, a successful businesswoman, heard God's Word from Paul, she *"opened her heart to respond,"* and she and her entire household became believers. Lydia opened her home and offered hospitality to Paul and his companions.

Later, when Paul and Silas had returned from prison, Lydia welcomed them into her home again and assisted them in their ministry. She hosted the first Christian church service in Philippi, and her home became a regional center of Christian outreach and worship—the first church in that area.

Rev. Choi said that he'd had a vision for Steven. "Don't be afraid of going," he said. "In the prison there will be a Lydia waiting for you. He will help you." He then prayed that God would provide Steven with someone who could assist with his evangelical work.

Steven prayed, "Lord, who is going to be my Lydia?" He didn't know where he was going or who would be there when he arrived.

On a Thursday near midnight, Steven was awakened from sleep and pulled from his cell. His hands and feet were handcuffed and shackled, and he was chained with heavy iron links to another prisoner, dragged out through the front gate, and shoved into a waiting black van. For the next ten hours, he sat bound upright without food, water, or a toilet as the van traveled north to his destination: Tiebe Prison in Changchun City, the huge industrial capital of China's northeast Jilin Province.

Tiebe is but one small cog in China's enormous prison conglomerate of *laogai*—work camps modeled on the old Soviet gulags. One report from 1992 identified more than two thousand work prisons and another three thousand detention centers scattered throughout the country—yet the count is inconclusive, due to the hundreds of facilities kept secret, isolated, and hidden in remote provinces. Among them, human rights organizations estimate that between three million and almost seven million prisoners are being held.

Although the prisoners of these labor camps aren't kept in their cells 24/7, all of them are required by Chinese law, under penalty of death, to work without pay for the State, whether or not they have been sentenced. Forced labor and the slave-driven factories of the *laogai* are, in fact, the backbone of China's economy. Chinese prisons manufacture automobiles and trucks, tools and machines, textiles, ceramics, chemicals, plastics, cement, paper, furniture, and dozens of other products. Prisoners run farms and raise livestock, produce tea, mine coal and other minerals, mill steel, refine petroleum and chemicals, and build and repair roads and railroads. They deal in food processing, welding, wilderness development, cement-making, and lumber and paper milling.

Prisoners are also used for medical tests and other forms of experimentation. Those imprisoned in remote areas have, for instance, been sent into nuclear bomb test sites before, during, and after explosions, to examine the effects of radioactivity on humans.

Each prison is responsible for its own economy; profits from production pay for staff salaries and other camp operations. Likewise, each prisoner is responsible for a predetermined level of individual production, with food and other "privileges" rationed according to his output—and cut off if his efforts are less than satisfactory. Those who fail to meet their production quotas often receive sentence extensions or are placed in solitary confinement. Some are beaten by guards and fellow prisoners, confined to handcuffs and shackles for days at a time, or tied naked to outdoor poles, exposed to the elements.

The organization of each *laogai* is modeled on the military. Supervision and surveillance are constant, and punishment for even the most minor of infractions is swift and brutal. Prisoner trustees supervise other inmates, meting out their own rations and treatment, depending on performance—and are often more repressive than the guards.

Laogai prisoners are given few clothes and almost no protection from cold temperatures or harsh environments. Anything beyond the most basic coverings must be purchased by the prisoner or sent in by his family. This means that those prisoners who have no outside support or sources of income, like the North Korean refugees, suffer.

Food rations in the *laogai* are kept to the bare minimum required for survival; typically, prisoners receive a bit of rough corn meal or bread, sorghum, a thin weed broth, and a little oil—no meat, fish, eggs, or vegetables. Some prisons offer once-a-month specials of a bun, meat broth, or wheat cakes; they may also treat inmates to a few dumplings on national holidays.

As a result of the low rations, prisoners suffer from constant illness, hunger, and malnutrition. And it is not uncommon for theft and violence to arise over food.

Most prisons are infested with rats, snakes, and insects, especially bed-bugs and lice. Driven by hunger, prisoners make every attempt to catch rats and snakes to eat, or to dig down into rat holes to recover whatever food the rats may have stored there.

Few prisons have hot water, let alone shower facilities; prisoners generally had to wash in cold water running from a row of faucets or at an outside well. Water quality, especially in industrial facilities, is usually poor and often polluted, with a foul taste and smell.

Conditions at the *laogai* are kept as secret as possible from the public and press. Reports inevitably leak out when prisoners are released, but photography is forbidden, even outside the prison perimeters, and violators are subject to immediate beatings and arrest.

Inmates in Chinese prisons see few visitors, even though they are generally permitted a twenty- to thirty-minute visit once a month after the investigative stage of their trial is complete. The remote location of most prisons makes them difficult to access, and those brave enough to visit risk being ostracized and even officially sanctioned when they return home.

For years, China has had the highest criminal execution rate in the world, with twenty times as many executions as occur in all the other countries combined; this rate is 50 percent higher than that of the next-highest-ranked nation. In 2008 alone, an estimated 10,000 prisoners were executed in China, compared to 37 in the United States—quadruple the per capita rate.

Executions are sometimes held publicly to serve as a cautionary example to other prisoners. In recent years, however, there has been an increase in private and secret killings.

And the methods have changed, as well, with a primary reason being the sharp increase in one of the Chinese prison system's most profitable means of "production"—the harvest and sale of human organs. According to at least one human rights agency, 2,000 to 3,000 organs a year are harvested in China and sold, 90 percent of them from executed prisoners.

In 1984, China formally acknowledged—and sanctioned—the long-standing practice of prisoners "donating" organs. The frequency of organ transplants rose dramatically around that time, due to the development of cyclosporine, a drug that helps control foreign-tissue rejection.

Technically, China's 1984 "Temporary Rules Concerning the Utilization of Corpses or Organs from the Corpses of Executed Prisoners" allows for the removal of prisoners' organs under only three conditions: (1) if the body is unclaimed, (2) if the prisoner consents, or (3) if the prisoner's family consents. Yet these guidelines are rarely followed.

Chinese cultural tradition dictates that, in the funeral process, a deceased body must be kept whole; therefore, voluntary organ donation is rare, not widespread, as it is in the U.S. And it is even less likely for the family of the deceased to volunteer his or her corpse. According to one account from a former deputy commander with the Public Security Bureau, not once in ten years of service did he ever hear of a prisoner giving permission for his organs to be used after his execution.

In 1993, the export of organs from China to anywhere but Hong Kong was outlawed, but it is not difficult to procure organs and undergo transplant within China itself, for Chinese and foreigners alike. It is common knowledge that high-ranking Chinese officials in the military, prison system, and government are favored as recipients.

It has long been a standard practice in Chinese prisons to schedule executions in order to accommodate the needs of paying organ recipients, but there have even been documented cases of organs being harvested from prisoners while they were still alive. One account details the story of a Chinese doctor summoned to a prison to remove both of a prisoner's kidneys the day *before* the man was scheduled to be executed. The "donor" was still alive, under anesthesia. The same night, the report added, at the same prison, eight kidneys were removed by four surgical teams, at least two of them supposedly earmarked for a high-ranking military official.

Hospital doctors confirm that prisoners' bodies are sometimes bought whole, so that a variety of organs and tissue may be put to use. The "leftover" remains are then cremated so that the victims' families cannot tell how the bodies were treated.

The profits from organ harvesting are enormous. The going rate (in U.S. dollars) in the mid-1990s, especially for wealthy foreigners, was $30,000 for a liver, $20,000 for a kidney, and $5,000 for a pancreas or a pair of corneas. The full procedure required $30,000 for tests, $30,000 for medicine, $100,000 for the operation, and $35,000 for follow-up treatment—a total of up to $200,000, payable at the time of the procedure. Cooperating hospitals, doctors, prisons, and prison officials all share in the profits.

The success rate for transplants from Chinese prisoners has been advertised as quite a bit higher than the international norm. It takes only one or two weeks to procure a kidney, so the risk to the recipient is reduced. Typically, the patient undergoes treatment at a hospital near the prison where the donor is being held; since the organ is fresh, the acceptance and survival rates are much higher. The prisoners targeted for execution and harvesting are also, by design, likely to be younger and healthier, and inmates are examined regularly for their suitability as donors. As a result of all these advantages, in China, the rate of kidney failure, for instance, is only a quarter of what it is in the U.S.

Transplant patients are told explicitly that the organs they receive are from prisoners. Ironically, as is true for all executions conducted in Chinese prisons, the prisoners' families are fully responsible for all related costs, including cremation and/or funeral expenses—as well as the bullet used in the execution.

The practice of organ harvesting has made execution techniques less "messy." For many years, the preferred method of execution was a rifle shot to the head with an expanding, hollow-point bullet. With corneas being one of the most sought-after body parts, it became necessary to use an alternate tactic to avoid damaging the marketable goods—namely, a pistol shot to the heart or, increasingly, lethal injection.

Steven had heard gruesome accounts from the *laogai* and expected the worst. The detention house had sold him to the Tiebe prison authorities in a virtual slave auction for the equivalent of just over $120, which was the going rate for a relatively strong, healthy, middle-aged male prisoner. *A hundred dollars*, he marveled, when told of his price. *That's all I'm worth to them. And they accuse me of human trafficking!*

Tiebe's geographical location provided a tough environment. There was no relief from the blazing heat and humidity of summer, and no hot water to warm them in the subzero temperatures and frequent whiteouts of the harsh winters in northern China.

The prison held 3,800 inmates, divided into twenty-three different units of at least 150 prisoners, with each unit responsible for earning an income working in the factory. The Tiebe facility produced electronics, facial tissues, arts and crafts products, paintings, furniture, clothing, and toys, all scheduled for shipment to domestic and foreign wholesalers, with the biggest buyers ordering from South Korea and America.

Prisoners preassembled thousands of pieces bound for low- and mid-end American stores. The quality and cleanliness of the products reflected the prisoners' lack of training and ability, as well as the abysmal prison conditions. Apathy was widespread, and it came across in negligent work and even deliberate tampering. Prisoners handled the merchandise with filthy fingers.

Not every prisoner was indifferent, however—Steven saw one inmate place a small note in a box that had been filled with toothpicks, labeled for Korea. "Don't use this," the man had written. "This is made in prison. It is dirty."

14

LYDIA

*"Unless the Lord had given me help,
I would soon have dwelt in the silence of death."*
—Psalm 94:17

Steven was assigned to the prison's twelfth unit, along with former high-ranking government officials and other new arrivals. On his second day, he heard a man call his name from outside his cell. *Who would call my name?* he wondered. *I just got here and I don't know anyone.* When he was brought out, he was met by a fully uniformed police officer, a unit guard.

"Are you the American?" the guard demanded in Chinese.

"Yes," Steve replied, "I am."

"Then you're the one I'm looking for."

The guard had heard that an American had just been admitted—the only one in the entire prison. And he wanted him as an English teacher.

Teaching English—not working in the factory—would be Steven's prison job. It was a mercy in many ways. Not only would Steven be exempt from laboring at factory work, but no one would disturb him. The guards at Tiebe were like gods. With no visitors to observe their behavior, they were free to treat the prisoners however they liked, beating and even killing them at will. But no guard would kill his own teacher—not after waiting so long for the opportunity to learn English.

Every morning, Steven would stand by until the guard summoned him to his office, usually around a quarter after seven. Then, the two would speak in English for an hour or so, the guard practicing his conversation skills, until 8:30, when he was scheduled to report to his post.

That was all Steven had to do. He knew he probably had the easiest job in the whole prison.

Steven had done a lot of devotional reading in the detention center, but one book had been especially important for him: *The Purpose-Driven Life* by Rick Warren. Helen had sent it, and he'd read it three times, cover to cover. The book had made a significant impact on Steven's thoughts about Christian living, and he had always tried to include its principles as part of his preaching to other prisoners.

Now, Steven was preaching not only to the prisoners but also to the guard he'd been tutoring in English. The guard had learned that Steven was a Christian preacher, and they sometimes discussed Steven's beliefs, if only for something else to discuss in English. At the end of their session one day, after they had been meeting together for about a month, Steven asked the guard what he thought about his beliefs—if he, too, wanted to believe, accept Christianity, and invite Jesus Christ to be his Savior.

"No," the guard said. "I don't."

"Why not?" Steven asked. "I can tell you're interested. What's holding you back?"

"Well, for one thing, I don't believe that Jesus really performed all the miracles you talk about. I mean, they make for good stories, but I don't think they were really true. If I saw them with my own eyes, maybe it would be different, but, without some proof, I can't accept them as real. If you could show me an actual miracle—really show me—maybe then I would believe."

Good, very good! Steven thought. "I understand," he said.

And with that, they parted, Steven walking back to his cell.

That night, Steven could hardly sleep. He kept thinking about how to reach the guard—how to preach to him, convince him, and help him believe in Jesus and God's miracles.

The next morning, he came to their session prepared. "Why do you think we're born on this earth?" he began, initiating the day's English conversation.

"I don't know," the guard said. "Why?"

"To please God," Steven answered, "because He is our Father. And, just like our sons should want to please us as fathers, so, too, should we try in everything we do to please God. That's why we are here.

"God is Father to all of us," Steven continued. "We are all His children. And since we are all born into God's family—all His children—we are all brothers and sisters."

"Everyone?" the guard asked, skeptical.

"Yes," replied Steven, "everyone."

"Even our enemies? Even beggars? Even the criminals in this prison?"

"Everyone," Steven repeated, "even the worst men in here."

"Okay," the officer said. But Steven could tell that he hadn't quite accepted his point. "What would that mean? Do we have to like each other?"

"Ha!" Steven laughed, thinking of some of his cell mates. "That's not very likely. But that doesn't mean we're not in the same family. And in a family, how should we act toward each other—even if we don't like each other? As brothers and sisters, what should we do?"

Now the guard just looked at him, waiting.

"We should support each other, help each other. And this will please our Father. This is the purpose of life."

"But how do we *know* what to do?" the guard persisted.

"That's why God sent His Son," Steven told him. "That's why we have Jesus Christ as our teacher, our model—to tell us and show us what to do. In order to please the Father, we have to follow the Son. We hear what Jesus said, see what He did, and follow His instructions of words and deeds. We should try to become more like Him, to do as He said and as He did.

"And just see—Jesus came to earth not to be served by other people but to serve *them*. We can see His service, again and again. So, that is what we, too, should do, how we should live—we should devote our lives to serving other people. In these ways—by pleasing God and being members of God's family and having Jesus as our model and serving others—we are also serving God.

"And, finally, once we can understand Jesus' lessons and live by them, we should tell other people—spread God's Word.

"Then, it all comes around in a circle: God will be pleased. That is why we are born; that is our purpose. That is why we are here on this earth!"

"Hmm," the guard considered. "I hadn't thought of it that way. But, you know, I still don't really believe. Talk is cheap. I still have to see a miracle with my own eyes; you still have to show me."

"Okay," Steven agreed. "I can accept that." He paused for a moment, trying to gauge how far he could push this man. Then, he thought about what he had learned in Father School.

The previous Sunday afternoon, Steven had been surprised to be called to the guard's office. "What are you doing here today?" Steven had asked him. "Aren't you off today?"

The guard had sat in his chair with his head down and an unhappy look on his face. Steven had sensed that something was wrong.

"What has happened?" Steven had asked. "What's the matter?"

"I've had a fight with my wife," the guard had started, and he'd gone on to tell Steven what had happened. Earlier that morning, his wife had been cleaning the house while he had been relaxing, just hanging around, on his day off. She had gotten angry with him, calling him lazy and accusing him of never helping her around the house. They had fought bitterly, and in the heat of the argument, he had stormed out of the house.

He'd been furious, but he'd also been hurt. He hadn't known what to do, where to go. So, he'd come to the only other place he knew—the place where he worked. The prison. Still fuming, he'd called for Steven, just to have someone to talk to. His marriage was a mess, he'd told Steven; his wife wanted a divorce.

Steven had talked the guard down from his anger, but now, several days later, he knew that the real cause of the fight hadn't been addressed and that the guard and his wife were still having problems.

"Do you love your wife?" he began. "Is your marriage still important to you?"

"Yes," the guard replied, "it is. I do love her."

"Do you ever tell her?" Steven asked.

"I'm not sure," the guard said. "Maybe not. I guess not."

"Okay," Steven continued, "then, here's what I want you to do; I have some homework for you: Write down twenty reasons why you love your wife. You write that out, and then, tomorrow, we'll look them over and talk about them."

The next day, when Steven was called to the morning lessons, the guard was waiting with a list written out in English. "Here are thirteen reasons," he said. "That's all I could think of."

"Okay, that's good," Steven assured him. He remembered how hard it had been for him to complete the full list when he'd been at Father School. "Tell me, do you and your wife ever do things together, just the two of you? Go out to dinner or anything like that?"

"Not anymore," the guard said, "not since we've been married."

"Okay," Steven told him. "That's your next assignment. I want you to take your wife out on a date. Take her to the best restaurant you can afford—one that suits her taste, whatever she would like. Ask her where she wants to go and take her there—just the two of you, without your children, without anyone else."

"All right," the guard said. "I can do that."

"Then, when you're sitting across from her in the restaurant," Steven instructed him, "I want you to confess your love to her. Bring this paper and read to her the thirteen reasons for your love."

"Then what?" the guard wondered.

"Then you'll see," Steven replied. "You might be surprised."

Steven didn't see the guard again for a few days. He started to worry. He wondered what had happened—how the date had gone.

The following Monday morning, Steven was again summoned to the guard's office for his English lesson. "So, what happened on your date?" he asked the guard as soon as they were alone. "How did it go?"

The guard smiled, almost shyly. "She was shocked," he said. "She couldn't believe it. And she was so touched. When I was reading the reasons, she had to hide her face, and I could tell she was crying. 'Is this really you?' she asked me when I finished reading all the reasons. 'What in the world has come over you? What has happened?'

"So, I told her about you—how I was taking English lessons from an American prisoner, and how you told me that if I wanted to win her back, if I wanted to reclaim her love, this is what I should do.

"'I didn't know whether to believe him,' I told her, 'but here we are—I'm trying it. What do you think?'

"She was so happy. 'I love you, too,' she said. 'I can hardly believe this. Maybe it's not too late for us, after all.'

"We didn't even stay till the end of dinner," the guard told Steven with a sheepish grin. "The children were staying at her parents' house, and we went home and had the place to ourselves. And you know what? She doesn't want to get a divorce anymore! She says I'm like an entirely new man, a new husband.

"Steven, you saved my marriage! I didn't think it was possible, but you did it—it worked!"

"Almost unbelievable," Steven suggested.

"Yes," the guard affirmed. "It's a miracle."

The guard's wife had been won over by the change she'd seen in her husband—how appreciative he was of her, how kind and attentive he'd become. And she, too, wanted to show her appreciation for this strange American from Korea who had brought about such enormous changes in her husband. Beginning the next day, every morning when Steven arrived for the English lesson, there was a fresh, homemade dish awaiting him in the office. Steven savored the delicious steamed dumplings and other delicacies, finding them all the more delicious for being gifts of gratitude for the work he had done with the guard. He wanted to save some of the food for his North Korean friends, but the guard wouldn't let him.

"They're for you," the guard insisted. "My wife is so thankful and told me I should watch as you ate it. She wants to meet you one day and cook for you in person.

"Plus, I told her about the other things we talk about—the teachings of Jesus and the Christian faith. She wants to hear more."

The survival of his marriage and the resurgence of a loving relationship with his wife was exactly the miracle the guard had required. Without another word of protest, he declared his commitment to the faith and to Jesus Christ as his Lord and Savior and was converted to Christianity.

After this pivotal moment, the English lessons took on a new tenor. Steven and the guard started reading the Bible and praying together every morning. They practically forgot that one of them was in prison behind bars, the other guarding the gates to keep him in. The New Testament was their textbook, and Steven's teaching integrated English language skills with spiritual lessons.

All of this had to be done in secret, of course, since such activities were strictly forbidden; the guard was in danger of losing not only his job but also his life. "Please don't tell anyone," he begged Steven at least once a week. "Don't mention my name—not to anyone. It would be the end of me."

"Don't worry," Steven assured him. "This is just between the four of us: you, me, your wife…and God. And He will protect you."

God had indeed sent Steven a Lydia—a helper, as well as his only contact with the outside world. Steven's lawyer had been permitted a rare visit, on occasion, to deliver letters—after they had been read and approved by the prison authorities. Other than that, he had no visitors. And while some prisoners, including the Koreans, were allowed two phone calls a month, Steven was denied this privilege due to being an American accused as a spy. In any case, the phones connected only to China and Korea—not to the U.S.

To get around the problem of Steven's isolation, the guard arranged to send Helen his office telephone number, along with the schedule of his sessions with her husband. When Helen called, the guard allowed Steven to talk to her and tell her what was happening to him, as well as to hear from her what was happening outside.

The guard also supplied Steven with books and anything else he needed from the outside world. He forwarded a letter to Steven's church in New York, requesting Bibles for Steven to distribute in prison. And he even rescued Steven's diaries and notebooks from Steven's cell and sent them to the Chang'an office. He was a true godsend—Steven's own Lydia.

15

WATER INTO WINE

"For you will go on before the Lord to prepare the way for him, to give his people the knowledge of salvation through the forgiveness of their sins, because of the tender mercy of our God, by which the rising sun will come to us from heaven to shine on those living in darkness and in the shadow of death, to guide our feet into the path of peace."
—Luke 1:76–79

*O*ne of the thirty-eight articles of law in the Chinese prison system prohibited any organized religious activity. If a prisoner wanted to worship, he had to do so by himself.

But Christians are not all monks, Steven thought defiantly. *We have to preach and worship together.* He meditated on his preaching thus far and marveled at its success. How was it, he wondered, that it had been so powerful, when his own knowledge was still so elementary, his level of realization not yet deep?

Then, he thought of Jesus' first miracle, at the wedding banquet in Cana—turning water into wine. When, Steven pondered, did the water actually become wine? First, the jars were filled with water. Then, Jesus directed the servants to draw some out and take it to the banquet manager. It wasn't until the water was drawn, Steven understood, that it became wine.

He related this truth to his preaching activities and learned an important lesson: when he drew the water and served it—when he delivered the Word of God to others—that was when it became "wine." *I must deliver*, he realized. *If it's not delivered, water remains water.* Whatever he heard and learned about the Word of God from his own teachers, he had to deliver to others. *Then it will become like the wine—powerful, life.* And if he wanted to keep learning, he had to teach.

Under the shelter of his association with his patron-guard, Steven had been praying and reading openly. Now he began to preach, and it didn't take long for his reputation as a Christian missionary and helper of refugees to spread throughout the prison, especially among the North Korean inmates—who, Steven knew, were desperate for hope.

There were more than a hundred North Korean refugee prisoners in Tiebe. Isolated from friends and family, they were made to suffer the worst of prison conditions. They had fled North Korea, where they were considered not only criminals but also traitors to the State and were subject to immediate execution. In China, they had led illegal lives underground. Their official status, as recorded on court papers and prison identification, was "nonnationals." They were unaffiliated, without any national legal status—without rights and without the protection of China, North Korea, or even international law.

As a result, they were commonly imprisoned and held for long periods of time—again, often before a trial, if one ever occurred. They were denied due process and thrown virtually anonymously into the maw of the Chinese penal system. Steven's American citizenship hadn't afforded him all the rights of process promised by Chinese law, but his position was better than that of the hopeless North Korean prisoners, who, even if they were released, would be handed over to North Korea, where they would face life sentences or execution, while their families were denied rations, jobs, or education and faced lives of humiliation as social pariahs.

The North Korean prisoners had no visitors at all. Even if a friend or family member had wanted to visit, he or she would not have been allowed out of North Korea; anyone who might have made it to China was far too poor. The refugee prisoners were given only five *yuán*—about seventy-five cents—a month. Without adequate money or sources of financial assistance, they couldn't afford to supplement the meager rations of food and clothing. Even toilet paper, which had to be purchased along with everything else, was beyond their means. Some sold their bodies in prison prostitution just to earn enough to survive. Others, if they were lucky enough, were able to earn a few *yuán* by doing laundry or performing other chores for the Chinese prisoners.

Yes, Steven knew that the North Koreans in Tiebe were suffering, and he recognized that they were yearning for faith. He longed to bring them together in worship and Bible study.

Because of the prisoners' heavy work schedule—up to twelve hours a day to make their quotas—they would have to meet early in the morning. So, Steven began holding prayer meetings at four in the morning.

There were no toilets in the cells in Tiebe—only in the common areas—so the cell doors were left unlocked, even at night. That meant that prisoners were free to go in and out of their cells, making early-morning gatherings possible.

Shortly before four o'clock every morning, Steven would get up, wash, and go to the adjacent cell to wake the North Korean refugee sleeping there. Together they would go to the next cell, and then the next, until they had gathered every member of their small group. All of them would then proceed to the washroom—Steven's prison church—and hold their daily session.

The men would pray together and sing Christian hymns Steven had taught them. He would read to them from the Bible and recount the stories of Jesus Christ. Within a week, the group's number doubled.

Again, because he was an American, Steven was housed in the same unit as higher-ranking prisoners. His unit was also the one to which prisoners were assigned upon admission; they remained there for at least three months, for training and adjusting to prison life, before being dispatched to another unit—one of the factories. This meant that Steven was able to reach every North Korean newcomer as soon as he arrived.

By law, Steven was allowed only three hundred *yuán*—about $45—every month; even though Chinese visitors smuggled in as much money as they could carry, anyone who visited Steven was kept to a stricter line. Steven's visibility as an American, and as an alleged spy, was a limiting factor when it came to contact with the outside world.

Inside the prison was a different story, however—once again, Steven's relationship with the guard paid off. The guard agreed to bring in money, which Helen would send every month, so that Steven could help the other prisoners. Inmates weren't allowed to carry cash, but they could draw from their account. So, instead of depositing all of the money from Helen into his own account, Steven would divide up the amount and make cash cards, giving a little to each of the members of his "church."

Commercially, the prison was like a small town, with a camp store that sold inmates the goods they needed. Whenever a North Korean prisoner was admitted into the unit, Steven would purchase him items for everyday use: a spoon, a bowl, a cup, a bar of soap, a towel, a toothbrush, a tube of toothpaste, a pair of socks, and a water container. He would also give each new arrival an allowance of a hundred *yuán* a month. Steven didn't allow the imprisoned refugees to spend the money on expensive luxury items, such as cigarettes, but, with his help, they were able to buy all of their basic necessities.

What the prisoners couldn't buy, they were sometimes able to have smuggled in. Among the most important items were audio lifelines to the world beyond the prison gates: transistor radios. Prisoners were not able to listen to broadcasts as a group—they would have attracted too much attention—but for half-an-hour, early each morning, after the prayer meetings and before wake-up, Steven and the others in his group would huddle under the covers or their beds like children, listening to the voices of Lee Won-Hee and Lee Soo-Kyung over Radio Free Asia, out of South Korea. And in the evenings, after bedtime, they heard William Kim from Voice of America.

When they reconvened the following morning, the men would discuss what they had heard—and the news was exciting. They discovered that people in the States and South Korea were talking about them. Freedom activists were working to further their cause on America's Capitol Hill. They had advocates in both the U.S. Senate and House of Representatives. Legislation had been passed—the North Korean Human Rights Act—to help improve conditions in North Korea and ease the plight of refugees. Furthermore, the American government was putting pressure on China to improve its record on human rights, end religious persecution, and release its political prisoners. Sometimes, guards would search their cells to find and confiscate the radios, but there were always more to be brought in. This cat-and-mouse game continued—the prisoners finding one way or another to tune into the broadcasts.

"I was so happy to hear their voices," Steven later recalled. "I feel like I can still hear them. People hadn't forgotten about us—or about the North Koreans. And they were working to get us free." These broadcasts filled the prisoners with hope and helped them to feel some sense of connection to their homes and to the rest of the world. As Steven remembers, "It felt like family."

When a prisoner's three months in the admittance unit were up, he was transferred into a different unit, where he would tell his friends about Steven's generosity. Steven quickly rose to fame among the prison population; the inmates came to view him as a benevolent godfather, both for his preaching and for his assistance, monetary and otherwise. As he had when he was helping refugees escape North Korea through China, he took care of the North Korean prisoners, watched out for them, and helped to make their lives as good as possible in prison. He developed a following throughout the center, and inmates would line up for an audience with him, each pleading his case, asking for some favor or a good word.

Naturally, Steven's attentions included the refugees' spiritual well-being. He continued his morning prayer meetings in the washroom. He also had his Korean church in Shenzhen send forty Bibles—translations in Chinese, Korean, and even English—to the home of his patron-guard, who brought them to the prison one at a time, smuggled in his lunch bag. He would deliver them to Steven during their daily English lesson.

Every day at lunchtime, to make more money, the prison kitchen sold the prisoners special meals—chicken, vegetables, or pork. During this period, they were allowed into an open field. Hundreds of inmates would mill about, affording Steven and his extended group, including those who had been transferred to other units, an opportunity to congregate together in one corner of the field for prayer and fellowship.

***

"At one time we too were foolish, disobedient, deceived and enslaved by all kinds of passions and pleasures. We lived in malice and envy, being hated and hating one another. But when the kindness and love of God our Savior appeared, he saved us, not because of righteous things we had done, but because of his mercy."
—Titus 3:3–5

One day in April, an infamous prisoner Steven had heard of came to see him in his cell. He was Chang Kwang-Jin, head of Korean-Chinese organized crime in the northeastern provinces. Chang was a cold-blooded murderer who had killed more people than he'd bothered to count or remember—and had plans to kill two more. He'd been arrested along with his whole inner circle—eighteen followers who would have laid down their lives for him in a moment—and had been given a life sentence. Everyone in Tiebe was afraid of him, prisoners and guards alike. He was an inmate, just like the rest; but, within those walls, he had free rein.

A few days earlier, a young prisoner from Steven's unit, a North Korean from his prayer group, had been transferred into Kwang-Jin's unit, and into his very cell.

"Teacher," Kwang-Jin addressed Steven—using the name many prisoners now called him—"one of your men has come into my cell, and he is always singing. He's always singing the same song, the same line, over and over again. 'Lord,' he sings, 'can I be forgiven—such a sinful man like me?' He's always repeating that, over and over, all the time—'Can I be forgiven, can I be forgiven, such a sinful man like me?' So I asked him, 'What is this gospel song you're always singing? Where did you learn it? Why do you keep singing like that?'

"And he said to me, 'Big brother, I learned it from my teacher. If you want to know about the song, you should go ask Mr. Teacher Kim.'

"So here I am, Mr. Teacher Kim, and I'm asking you, what is it with that song? What keeps this man singing it every day, singing that one line over and over again? And who is the Lord this boy is singing to, the one who has the power to forgive us? I've killed many men, Teacher. Do you think your Lord can forgive even a man like me?"

Steven looked at Kwang-Jin. So many men had met their deaths at this man's hands. Surely, all the fires of hell awaited him. And yet, here he was, placing himself before Steven and asking, "Who is the Lord?"

As he gazed into Kwang-Jin's eyes, Steven remembered Matthew 6:12: *"Forgive us our debts, as we also have forgiven our debtors."* He also thought of what Christ said while hanging on the cross: *"Father, forgive them, for they know not what they are doing"* (Luke 23:34). If Jesus could beg forgiveness for the very people who had crucified Him—even those who had tortured Him on His way to Calvary—wasn't there room for one more? Even this killer before him, Steven realized—even this murderer—was not beyond redemption.

Steven felt a surge of happiness. Here was a cold-blooded killer, a grievous sinner, asking him who the Lord was.

"Mr. Chang, may I please pray for you?" Steven requested.

"Okay," Kwang-Jin said. "I guess it can't do any harm."

"Give me your hands," Steven said. "Join me in my prayers."

Kwang-Jin placed his hands in Steven's. And Steven, forgetting where he was, the life he'd been leading in prison dissolving in a wash of compassion, knelt on the cold stone floor and pulled Kwang-Jin down with him. Seated face-to-face with Kwang-Jin, their hands between them, Steven closed his eyes and began, "Our Lord, who art in heaven, hallowed be Thy name. We come to You on bended knees, sinners through and through. Please, Lord, hear this man who seeks after You; hear this man who asks for Your grace. Please let him know You. Please have forgiveness on him, Lord, even after all his sins; please shine Your love on him and show kindness on his family."

For fifteen minutes, Steven spoke like this, praying to the Lord for Kwang-Jin, for his family, for the forgiveness of his sins—praying that Kwang-Jin would come to know God, surrender to Him, confess his own sins, and ask for forgiveness.

Tears flowed down Steven's cheeks, dripping from his chin onto the men's clasped hands. He felt as if he had never wanted anything more in the world than to pray for this one man's salvation.

At last, Steven concluded his prayer: "Amen." And when he finally opened his eyes, he felt as if he was seeing a new Chang Kwang-Jin before him.

Kwang-Jin's hands still held Steven's, now wet with his tears. With eyes open wide, he stared at Steven. "No one has ever cried for me before," he said. "What have I done to deserve your kindness, your prayers? And what can I do to earn the Lord's forgiveness?"

"All you have to do is humbly ask," Steven told him. "All you have to do is surrender to the Lord Jesus Christ—accept Him as your God and confess your sins. He is a loving Father, Kwang-Jin, and if you come to Him, He will take you into His heart."

"Really?" Kwang-Jin pressed, amazed. "That's all?"

"That's all," Steven affirmed. "And I know you'll find that if you give your love to the Lord, as well and open your heart to His, things will start happening differently for you. There is a beautiful psalm that says, *'I call with all my heart; answer me, O LORD, and I will obey your decrees. I call out to you; save me and I will keep your statutes. I rise before dawn and cry for help; I have put my hope in your word'* (Psalm 119:145–147).

"Why don't you think it over? We can talk more tomorrow. Then, I'll answer your question more fully and tell you about the Lord."

The next day, Kwang-Jin returned to Steven's cell. He came again, a few days later, and then regularly, twice a week. Each time, they would talk together for an hour or two, Steven preaching the gospel, reading from God's Word, and telling Kwang-Jin about the life everlasting.

One day, about a month after their first meeting, Kwang-Jin came to Steven and said, "Teacher, I'm ready. I want to accept the Lord. I'm ready to surrender."

"That's great," Steven said. "That's wonderful."

"But first, I have something I want to confess to you," Kwang-Jin said. "I've never told anyone about this; you're the first one.

"You really should be talking to God, not me," Steven told him. "I'm just a sinner like yourself, asking the Lord for His forgiveness."

"I understand," Kwang-Jin said. "But first, I need to tell someone who is standing right in front of me. First, I want to tell you.

"I killed two people before I came here," Kwang-Jin continued. "For those deaths, I was arrested and am being punished, here in Tiebe. But they were not the only victims on my list. There are two more people I'm still supposed to kill when I'm released. I'm not saved yet."

"Remember," Steven told Kwang-Jin, "Jesus Christ died for your forgiveness. Your salvation is in the blood that He shed for you. '*This is my blood of the covenant,*' He told His disciples, '*which is poured out for many for the forgiveness of sins*' (Matthew 26:28).

"Don't you think that if Jesus could forgive even a murderer like you, and die for your salvation, you can try to forgive these two poor souls, change the course of your life, and let them go—let them live?"

***

"Repent and be baptized, every one of you, in the name of Jesus Christ for the forgiveness of your sins. And you will receive the gift of the Holy Spirit."
—Acts 2:38

That very afternoon, in the corner of the exercise yard, Steven sprinkled water over Kwang-Jin's head and performed the rites of holy baptism. Tears streamed down both men's cheeks as Steven conducted the sacred ceremony, concluding, "...in the name of Jesus Christ, amen."

The next morning, earlier than their usual meeting time, Kwang-Jin burst into Steven's cell. "Teacher," he exclaimed, "you won't believe what happened last night! For the last twenty-two years, I haven't been able to sleep a single night straight through. Every night, I have terrible nightmares. I see the men I killed still running away from me, and others behind me, chasing me down.

But, last night, I slept all the way through; it was the most peaceful sleep of my entire life!

"You've cured me, Teacher Kim," he said. "What can I do to repay you?"

"I'm so happy for you, Kwang-Jin," Steven said with a smile. "But it wasn't me; it was Jesus Christ. It's just like I said—you're feeling the greatness of His love, the peace of His forgiveness.

"There's nothing you need to do to pay me; you don't owe me a thing. But the price of God's love is very high; it is our whole heart. Love Him and follow His commandments, Kwang-Jin, and you'll have peace for the rest of this life and for all eternity."

"Teacher," Kwang-Jin said, "thank you."

Kwang-Jin joined Steven's prayer group. He read the Bible every day and kept a prayer journal, bringing Steven one question after another to answer. And the fear that he had previously inspired in his fellow inmates was replaced with something altogether different—something that now inspired them to ask about the Lord. Every week, he brought another prisoner to Steven and said, "Teacher, tell this boy everything you told me. Tell him how he can be forgiven."

Kwang-Jin became Steven's number one recruiter. On Sundays, not only would he show up for prayer service; he would bring his entire following of criminals. Most important, Kwang-Jin gave up his life of crime and violence. He forgave those men who were still on his hit list, and vowed to follow Christ's law.

Later that spring, Steven heard that Kwang-Jin had been caught with a note to Steven in his possession. Steven couldn't understand; Kwang-Jin was so powerful. Such a minor infraction should not have been an issue; something must have happened. But he never found out. Kwang-Jin was transferred to another prison, and Steven never heard from him again.

Something had happened, but it wasn't in relation to Kwang-Jin; it was Steven. The protests in America were beginning to have an effect, and the Chinese government was reacting. Steven's name was being broadcast in the American media. Suzanne Scholte, chair of the North Korean Freedom Coalition, was championing his cause. Helen was writing to senators and congressmen, and their daughter, Lisa, was filmed at a protest in Washington, D.C., carrying her father's picture and a banner calling for his release, while calling out his name.

There was even talk of boycotting the Beijing Olympics, which would pose a direct and very real threat to the Chinese economy. Faced with a potential public-image fiasco and financial disaster, the Chinese government took quick action to condemn Steven by isolating him, meanwhile pressuring the prison authorities to curtail his activities.

They were aided by a Korean-Chinese prison "pastor" who had been arrested, ironically, for fraud—he'd collected thousands of dollars from North Korean refugees, only to abandon them in China. When the North Korean prisoners spurned him and followed Steven, his jealousy led him to cooperate with the authorities, giving them the names of Steven's Christian friends.

Steven was accused of being an American spy and forbidden to meet with any other prisoners. The guards harassed all of his known associates, apprehending them, beating them, and subjecting them to torture.

The prayer group was shattered. One evening, Steven slipped a book to one of the North Koreans, and the man was immediately taken and searched. The guards put a hood over his head, handcuffed him to a chair, and beat him with steel rods, well into the night. "What is this book?" they demanded. "Where did you get it?"

"It's nothing," the man begged. "It's just a book."

The book was in Korean, so the guards couldn't tell what it said, but they brought in a Korean-Chinese prisoner and ordered him to translate the title. "Is it a Christian book?" they questioned.

When they found out that it was, they hung the man by his wrists from a pole and left him out in the yard. In the morning, they dragged his limp body to a tiny solitary cell—no more than a box, really—where he was confined for fifteen days. The other prisoners got the message, loud and clear: anyone who spoke to Steven was risking his life.

Because Steven was an American, the authorities wouldn't kill him, torture him, or make him disappear. Still, they did just about all they could: locked him in solitary confinement for two months, made every attempt to toughen his sentence, and punished everyone around him. His privileges, including communication with the outside world, were revoked, and, despite a persistent cough that compelled him to make repeated protests, he was put in a cell where everyone smoked. The U.S. consul was the only visitor allowed—once every three months.

The crackdown put a stop to the prayer meetings, but neither Steven nor the others would give up. Instead of meeting together physically, they communicated via secret messages—letters concealed in empty coffee bags, stashed in hiding places, or passed along when no one was watching. The other prisoners were no longer permitted to keep a Bible in their possession, so Steven would write out verses—sometimes entire chapters—to help keep their devotional study alive. When he was outside for his daily half hour of exercise, he would find a stone on the outskirts of the field and slip these written pages underneath it. Later, a prisoner on his way to work would snatch the paper, hide it on his person, read it when he returned to his cell, and then leave it in a different hiding place for someone else to find. Thus, they were able to continue their fellowship, creatively and carefully.

Steven spent his time focusing on his own private devotions and delving deeper into Scripture. He read and prayed almost constantly, committing psalms and Bible verses to memory.

16

YANCHENG PRISON, BEIJING

November 21, 2005

"Wake up! Strengthen what remains and is about to die,
for I have not found your deeds complete in the sight of my God.
Remember, therefore, what you have received and heard; obey it, and
repent. But if you do not wake up, I will come like a thief,
and you will not know at what time I will come to you."
—Revelation 3:2–3

By the fall of 2005, Steven was well-known in America as a Chinese political prisoner, and his case was attracting a good deal of international attention. His treatment had even become a factor in China's plans to host a successful Summer Olympic Games in 2008, as well as to progress in their relations with the U.S. and the West. Steven had been in Tiebe prison for fifteen months, and to avoid any possible trouble, the authorities there wanted to get rid of him in any way they could.

On November 21, Steven was transferred from Changchun City to Beijing's Yancheng Prison, a facility managed directly by China's Department of Justice. Yancheng was known as China's premiere showcase unit, built by the government in early 2000 to demonstrate to visitors, foreign dignitaries, and the rest of the world how well China treated its inmates.

Yancheng bore little resemblance to the *laogai* or any other part of the Chinese prison system. It had a gym and a library for the prisoners to use. Not only were families allowed to visit the prisoners; they also were invited to spend time with them. And since there were visitors nearly every day, everything was kept neat and clean, including the prisoners themselves—finally, there was hot water for washing. Pointing to Yancheng, the Chinese government could proudly say, "Look at how well we treat even the criminal element of our society!"

Publicity photo of the prisoners at Beijing's Yancheng Prison; Steven (highlighted) is in the second row.

At Yancheng, Steven enjoyed privileges he'd almost forgotten. He took his first hot shower in two years and slept on a bed with a real mattress. He was even served fresh fruit and vegetables, milk, and eggs. His health improved, marked especially by a lowered blood pressure. But, while the basic amenities in Yancheng were the best Chinese prisons had to offer, there were fewer extras to be procured. In Tiebe, as an American with money and outside resources, Steven had been able to afford special food, clothing, and other privileges. In contrast, the Yancheng grocery was open only once or twice a month, and Steven, like the other inmates, was kept to the standard monthly allowance of 300 *yuán*—$45.

There were approximately 600 prisoners in Yancheng, but Steven's unit, reserved almost entirely for foreigners, held only forty. They came from sixteen countries around the world, including the U.S., Cameroon, Canada, Colombia, DR Congo, Ghana, Japan, Korea, Nigeria, the Philippines, Russia, Singapore, and Switzerland. They were a better class of prisoners than Steven had served with previously, as most of them had been jailed not for violent crimes but for political activities and financial infractions.

***

*"Have I not commanded you? Be strong and courageous.
Do not be terrified; do not be discouraged, for the LORD your God will be
with you wherever you go."*
—Joshua 1:9

There were many Christians in Yancheng, as well, making up almost half the foreign population. There was another pastor, too, a Korean-American named Peter Chang. On his first Sunday at Yancheng, Steven asked Chang what time services were held.

"We don't have any; we can't," Chang told him.

"How is that?" Steven asked. "We're Christians; we have to worship. Every Sunday we have to practice and strengthen our faith."

"We cannot," the pastor repeated. "We're not allowed."

Not satisfied with his answer or his explanation, Steven approached the unit's Korean elder, Lee Hee-Chul, but he, too, confirmed the pastor's statement: "No services." No Christian worship was permitted. And the rules of the prison were enforced with as much zeal as the physical conditions were kept polished and pristine: prisoners' activities were highly visible, and the ban on group religious practice was strictly enforced.

"Then, I'll just have to hold my own," Steven decided, "even if I'm the only one." In all of his months of incarceration, even in the harsh conditions of the old Yanji cells, Steven hadn't missed one day of worship, and he wasn't going to break his record. "If anyone wants to join me, they are very welcome."

That evening, when Steven knelt in worship in his cell, he was joined by two Koreans: Elder Lee and Brother Suh. *Only two*, he thought, *but it's a start.* He thought of Jesus' words to His disciples recorded in Matthew 18:20: *"For where two or three come together in my name, there am I with them."*

Elder Lee was serving a life sentence; Brother Suh was in for fifteen years for theft. As they talked together afterward, Steven could see the consequences of the spiritual inactivity in Yancheng. In the six years that Elder Lee had been imprisoned, he had neither held nor participated in even one Sunday service. The other Christians looked up to Steven, but, without regular community, Bible study, or worship, they had little understanding of Christian doctrine and almost no active faith—no sense that Christ was present in their lives.

The Christian prisoners in Yancheng, Steven saw, were simply afraid. Religious meetings were against prison regulations, and they feared reprisals from the authorities. In a way, the superior prison conditions had exacerbated the situation, because, with more privileges, the men had more to lose. But Steven had fought these same battles in the prisons where he'd previously been incarcerated, and though he had faced challenges and setbacks, he'd never backed down, nor had he never been defeated. As far as he was concerned, there was nothing to fear.

I have to do something, Steven decided. He had only just arrived in Yancheng, but the realizations he'd experienced since his arrest had confirmed for him that every day was important; there was no time to waste. He knew that he had to bring the men together to worship, but he also felt the need for something more. If he could encourage the men to pray, that was good. And it was even better if they could worship together in groups. But it still wasn't enough; he wanted the prisoners to become spiritually *active*—to engage them in activities that would help educate them, spiritually, and deepen their devotion. And doing so on Sundays alone wouldn't suffice; if anything significant was going to happen in the prison after so many years of spiritual stagnation—if they were going to conquer their fears and fully embrace the Lord—they would have to meet every day and actually *do* something.

The next afternoon, Steven spoke with the two inmates who had worshipped with him in his cell and got them to agree that on the following day, Tuesday, they would meet together for a prayer session and Bible study. As a venue, Steven suggested the library. The atmosphere there wasn't very conducive to religious contemplation—men sat around, talking and eating, and generally treated the place less like a library than a recreation room. But Steven hoped, and the men agreed, that all the activity would make their meeting less conspicuous. He chose a table in the corner, and the next evening, when their work was done, he sat with Elder Lee and Brother Suh to read, talk, and pray.

"Our first service was so moving," Steven remembered later. "There had been so much fear in the prison for so long, and here we were, worshipping in the library, out in the open. All three of us were crying; we were full of grace."

The two other men were a bit nervous, but they were also inspired and greatly enthused; they didn't want to let even one day go by without getting together again for religious study, community, and worship.

So, on Wednesday, the three men gathered once more around the corner table in the library. But their previous get-together had not gone unnoticed by the guards, and the authorities had prepared a response. When the men began their informal service, they immediately sensed tension in the room. Suddenly, a uniformed guard—a high-ranking officer—marched through the door and confronted the men at their table. "What are you doing?" he shouted. "This is a prison! Return to your cells immediately!"

Steven witnessed no beatings in Yancheng, no torture—it was, after all, the showcase of Chinese prisons—but the authorities still enforced the rules; the officer threatened the men that if they did not comply, they would be sorry. There was little the officer could do to Elder Lee—he was there for life—but he threatened Steven and Brother Suh that if they didn't follow the prison rules, their sentences could be extended.

Without another word, the three men rose from their seats and returned to their cells. On Thursday, having discussed the possibilities and weighed the risks, they tried to meet again in a different room, but the authorities were ready; there was no way they could continue unobserved. The library, as well as most of the other rooms in the prison, had surveillance cameras, and the guards had hired other prisoners to keep a close eye on Steven and anyone who talked to him or befriended him in any way. The hired prisoners' watch was vigilant—twenty-four hours a day—and whatever they saw, they reported.

"Okay," Steven told the two men. "Obviously, this isn't going to work. But we can't just stop; we have to try something else.

"What makes us most visible?" he asked them. "How can the guards and authorities tell what we're doing? It has to be the books and the meetings. We'll have to manage without them. Somehow we have to study the Bible, but without Bibles. We have to sing, but without hymnals. And we have to get together, but without looking like we are having a meeting.

"From now on, we'll have to worship and study from memory. We have to memorize the verses and songs so we can recite and discuss and sing them without referring to the text. And we can't have a meeting place. Instead of sitting together in our cell or around a table, wherever we are, that's where we'll hold our meeting; that will be our church. If we're walking in the yard, we'll act as if that's all we're doing—just walking and chatting. But that will be our prayer session. If we're eating or washing or working—whatever we're doing, anywhere—we'll turn that into our worship service. If we play this right, no one will be able to tell if we're worshipping and sharing our realizations about the Lord, or complaining about yesterday's breakfast."

It was a great idea, the other men agreed. They had never heard anything like it.

For the next several weeks, Steven did everything he could to memorize Bible verses. He wrote key phrases on scraps of paper and on his palms. Throughout the day, he repeated those verses to himself, over and over, and sang hymns under his breath. Every night, he fell asleep murmuring psalms and lessons from the Gospels. It was hard for him—he'd always had the benefit of notes and had never been good at memorization—but, eventually, he had committed enough to memory that he could resume teaching and leading the others in prayer.

From then on, from the viewpoints of the guards and other prisoners, Steven and his companions always seemed to have something to talk about. Wherever they might be, they could always be seen deep in discussion. But they weren't actually "meeting," and they never had books with them, so they didn't seem to be breaking any prison rules, and the guards left them alone.

Steven's informal, mobile services continued through the winter. The group's success lifted the spirits of Steven and the other men, and they derived even a bit more satisfaction knowing that they were worshipping right under the watchful eyes of the guards, surveillance cameras, and hired spies.

When the other Christian prisoners saw that Steven and his two companions were suffering no consequences, they felt encouraged, and some decided to join in. One at a time, without ceremony, prisoners added themselves to the group's "walking church." And the other two original members, following Steven's example, also committed verses and songs to memory. More men than ever were taking to the Word of God, and Steven was overjoyed.

With the group meetings apparently having been nipped in the bud, surveillance relaxed, and, over time, the authorities' harassment of the Korean Christians also lessened. Eventually, they were able to worship together and sing aloud without attracting undue attention. The officer who had broken up the library service had disappeared; Steven heard that he'd had a stroke and had been forced to retire. And another prison official who had been antagonistic toward the group also suffered a disabling accident. Word got around the prison: if anyone tried to interfere with the Christian worship group, God would punish him.

The walking worship and bookless Bible studies soon became unnecessary. The group now met openly, and no one, not even the guards, dared to bother them or disrupt their gatherings. Whenever they congregated, the guards would seem to disappear, returning to their posts after the services were over. Besides the rumors that those who harassed the group would experience misfortune, Steven found out, there was also a delegation of Chinese dignitaries scheduled to make a prison visit. Wanting everything in the prison to be as peaceful as possible, the authorities had loosened some of the rules restricting prisoner privileges.

For the next eight months, the group sang and worshipped undisturbed. As more Korean prisoners joined them, the group branched out, and there were soon three Korean congregations within the unit of foreigners. Early every morning, before work, they had Bible class. Under Steven's guidance, the men studied the New Testament from beginning to end. Steven introduced them to other books and ideas, too—Rick Warren's *Purpose-Driven Life* and the works of Charles Stanley. They used the gospel of John to focus their meditations. From noon until one thirty, during the daily rest period, they would gather to pray, read, and share their experiences and realizations.

Until that time, their worship and discussion had been conducted entirely in Korean, but Steven began to consider the possibility of spreading the ministry to the English-speaking prison population, as well. He translated the Bible verses and Christian readings from Korean and started conducting two separate services, one in Korean and one in English. Four prisoners—from the Philippines, Singapore, DR Congo, and Cameroon—joined almost immediately.

Preaching and leading services in English was a new experience for Steven—and a time-consuming one, as well—and he found himself praying a lot for guidance. More inmates joined the services, and before long, ten English-speaking men were worshipping together. The wife of one of the men, a Methodist from Hong Kong who was active in prison ministry, visited monthly and brought English Bibles and other spiritual books. She also sent them an English worship program, which they used to structure their services. Steven had created an international parish within the prison walls.

That spring, Steven read about a prison group in the Middle East who, by saving bread and water, had introduced Communion services to their worship. *What a great idea*, he thought. He wanted to use wine, but liquor was forbidden in the prison. Once, they managed to purchase some grapes and tried making wine. During the process, however, they were discovered and stopped by the guards. Finally, Steven had Helen send him packages of powder for making instant grape juice. One Sunday in May, worshipping in Korean in the morning and in English in the afternoon, the Yancheng Christian prisoners held their first Communion service.

17

LABOR

"Come to me, all you who are weary and burdened,
and I will give you rest. Take my yoke upon you and learn from me,
for I am gentle and humble in heart, and you will find rest for your souls.
For my yoke is easy and my burden is light."
—Matthew 11:28–30

The authorities in Yancheng remained more tolerant of various prisoner activities, Steven found, as long as the men fulfilled their production quotas. The conditions in Yancheng were far less harsh than they had been in Tiebe, but it was, after all, still part of the Chinese work-prison system.

For his first month in Yancheng—his adjustment period—Steven hadn't been given any work. But now, from 8:00 until 11:30 in the morning and from 1:30 until 5:00 in the afternoon, he had to labor in the prison factory making silk flowers—which, like most of the merchandise produced in the prison, were bound for American chain stores.

Flower-making was a hot job. Steven and the other workers had to burn the silk with candles and then glue the flowers together—thousands of pieces per day. There was no protection or relief from the toxic fumes that filled the small, unventilated room; even in the heat of summer, no fans could be used because they would extinguish the lit candles. Steven tried wearing a cloth mask over his mouth and nose, but the room was already so stifling that he was just trading one discomfort for another.

One of the Korean inmates, Suh Jung-Min, told Steven that he had worked in the paper factory in Tianjin prison, making little red boxes for McDonald's Happy Meals. *Ironic*, Steven thought. How many times had Helen taken the children to McDonald's for food packaged in those very boxes? It was possible that they had eaten from a box in Long Island that Suh Jung-Min had cut to size in Tianjin.

Steven couldn't help but think about life back in the States, where so many people focused all their attention on material possessions—on accumulating wealth and buying new things. He remembered how, for so many years, those things had been his own focus. He meditated on the warning in Matthew 6:24 that one could not serve two masters, both God and money, and reminded himself of the exhortation that followed: *"Seek first his kingdom and his righteousness, and all these things will be given to you as well"* (Matthew 6:33).

The success of the prison ministry gladdened Steven enormously, but it also demanded a lot of time and effort. Each Sunday, he delivered two sermons for which he prepared all week. As soon as he was done with the English sermon on Sunday afternoon, he immediately began thinking about what he would preach the following week. Monday through Wednesday, he would read through the Bible and meditate on what to say. Usually, the group readings would follow a sequence, but, on Sundays, he tried to make his sermons relevant to what was going on in their lives. On Thursdays and Fridays, he would write his sermons—one in Korean and one in English. Saturdays were his recital days; he would reread the sermons aloud to himself, over and over again—ten or twenty times—until he had memorized them both. He meditated on the words, trying to find deeper revelations, and practiced his delivery in order to achieve the best effect. *Pastors Won and Cho were naturals at this,* Steven remembered admiringly. *I have to work so hard just to get my words to come out right!*

Steven was so focused on ministry that he had little time or patience for anything else. His labors in the silk flower factory were an almost unbearable interruption. He would complete only as much work as he had to, and then immediately return to studying, learning more psalms, putting together hymnals for the other prisoners, and preparing his sermons for the Sunday services.

Prison terms in China are based on a point-reduction system. Sentences are often set at a length disproportionately large for the crime, in order to give the prisoners more motivation to work in hopes of reducing their sentence. In the American prison system, prisoners are rewarded reduced time for good behavior; in China, they have to earn points—equating to off their sentences—either by bribing the right official or by laboring harder and producing beyond their quota.

By earning points, prisoners could reduce their terms by as much as a year. Generally, however long the deduction, twice as much time was required working to earn it. To accumulate six months' credit, a prisoner had to work one year; to earn a year's worth, he had to work two.

When Steven entered Yancheng, he already had been imprisoned for over two-and-a-half years, with almost the same amount of time still left to serve. He learned that by producing just a little more than his minimum quota, he would almost automatically earn the points necessary to get the maximum deduction and cut his time in half.

He was transferred to the hardware factory, where he hammered nails into plastic clips that would be used in home-assembly shelves. At this point, he was still fulfilling the minimum quota—he completed 2,000 pieces a day, but hardly any more.

One afternoon, on his way out of the factory, he stopped to talk with one of the foreign prisoners who labored near him. The man's method, Steven had noticed, was almost diametrically opposed to his own: he always arrived at the factory early and stayed until closing.

Oki San was a sixty-six-year-old Buddhist antique dealer from Japan. He had been visiting China on a buying trip, he told Steven in poor English, wandering through an open-air flea market, when he had seen a small, twelve-piece china tea set displayed on a table. It wasn't the kind of thing he typically looked for, but he'd thought his wife might like it; and so, after negotiating a better price for the set, he had wrapped it up to bring back for her as a gift. As Oki was making his way home, airport security had searched through his belongings, pulled out the china tea set, and arrested him. He'd been charged with, and later convicted of, smuggling a Chinese "national treasure." And he'd been given a life sentence.

Prison life was hard for Oki. Since he was Japanese, he was despised by both the Koreans and Chinese, prisoners and guards alike. No one would go out of his way to do anything for him.

Oki wasn't a Christian, so he and Steven hadn't prayed together or formed much of a bond, but Steven felt compassion for the aging Buddhist. After all, Oki hadn't knowingly done anything wrong, and now he was likely to spend the rest of his life in prison. "Is there anything I can do?" Steven asked him. "How can I help?"

Oki told Steven that his goal was to be released before he died. "I'm working as hard as I can," he said. He often completed 10,000 pieces per day to earn his maximum allowable points, but it still wasn't enough.

Starting the following morning, every day for a week, Steven worked an extra hour for Oki after finishing his own quota.

"Thank you so much," Oki said to him. "I can't tell you how much I appreciate it. I guess Christians aren't as bad as I thought."

Steven was struck by Oki's remark. He had never imagined that someone could think of Christians as being anything other than wonderful people. Then, he remembered how his fellow Korean prisoners treated Oki. *Maybe sometimes, just being Christian isn't enough,* he realized. For some reason, he recalled Moon, his Buddhist cell mate in Yanji. Steven had tried to convert him to Christianity, he remembered; and, for a while, Moon had joined him in prayer. But when Steven had pressed him to give up his Buddhist beliefs and practices, Moon had resisted; in the end, Steven's pressure had pushed Moon away. *Maybe I was too hard on him,* Steven thought. *Maybe sometimes, people have to find their faith in different ways.*

He thought of Jesus' words of comfort from John 14:1–2: *"Do not let your hearts be troubled,"* He had told His disciples. *"In my Father's house are many rooms."*

Humbled, Steven wondered for the first time if there might not be rooms in the kingdom of God for souls like Moon and Oki, too. *"No one comes to the Father except through me"* (verse 6), Jesus had continued, but Steven wondered whether there were many paths leading to Christ. And, once again, he suspected that no matter how hard or how long he studied Scripture, he would never fully understand God's plans.

18

THE FINAL STRETCH

August 2007

"We will support you, so take courage and do it."
—Ezra 10:4

As the days and weeks passed, Steven started looking forward to his own release. There were still almost fourteen months left on his sentence, but if everything went well, it would be reduced, and he would be able to get out in a couple of months. By working harder in the factories like his friend Oki, Steven eventually earned enough points for a full year's sentence deduction, and he had submitted his application through the proper authorities.

On the outside, from their home in Long Island, Helen had continued her relentless campaign for Steven's release. She sent urgent appeals to human rights organizations and pro-democracy groups, contacted U.S. officials, and did everything else she could to rally public opinion in favor of her husband and put more pressure on the government to take action.

With the help of her attorney and Suzanne Scholte, Helen had written letters to congressmen Henry Hyde, of Chicago's North Side, and Ed Royce, of California; to her Long Island congressman, Steven Israel; and to senators Richard Lugar of Indiana and Joseph Biden of Delaware. She had urged New York senators Hillary Clinton and Charles Schumer to take swift, decisive action. She had sent impassioned messages to President George W. Bush and former President Jimmy Carter. When she failed to receive the desired response, she had followed up these pleas with further calls and written appeals. She sent three-page faxes to Representative Israel and senators Schumer and Clinton, restating her request that they write to China on Steven's behalf.

Senator Lugar, then chairman of the Senate Foreign Relations Committee, had responded by writing a letter to the Chinese ambassador, asking that Steven be treated as the humanitarian he was and that his sentence be reduced. The State Department had also sent an internal memo to its Beijing office expressing concern over Steven's case, and officials from the U.S. Embassy in Beijing had then filed a diplomatic request on Steven's behalf with China's Ministry of Foreign Affairs, seeking early parole.

Following this request, senators Clinton and Schumer had written to James Kelly, Assistant U.S. Secretary of State for East Asian and Pacific Affairs, requesting that the federal branch of the United States government urge China to give Steven's case special consideration. "Dear Mr. Kelly," they had written, using the U.S. Senate letterhead:

> We are writing to request the Department of State's attention with respect to Mr. Seung Whan Kim...a United States citizen residing in New York who was arrested by Chinese authorities in September 2003 for assisting North Korean citizens in China....

> It is our understanding that in June 2004, the U.S. Embassy in Beijing communicated to the Chinese Ministry of Foreign Affairs that Mr. Kim has admitted his guilt and has expressed sincere regret that his actions violated Chinese law, explaining that he took these actions solely for humanitarian reasons....

> We would like to express our support for this communication and respectfully urge you to underscore to Chinese officials the importance

of ensuring that Mr. Kim's pending appeal receives full consideration and all due process available under Chinese law, and that humanitarian factors be given all due consideration as well.

One of Steven's most outspoken advocates was Suzanne Scholte, chair of the North Korean Freedom Coalition and Defense Forum Foundation. She had written her own letters of appeal to Congressman Israel and senators Clinton and Schumer. Most visibly, she had helped rally public support and organized protests and demonstrations, including the one in Washington, D.C., where Helen and the Kims' daughter, Lisa, had shown Steven's picture and read out his name.

Steven—and all of the North Korean prisoners—received their strongest Senate support from Sam Brownback of Kansas, a member of the Senate Appropriations Committee and chairman of the Senate Relations Subcommittee on East Asia and Pacific Affairs. Senator Brownback had personally visited China, spending three days in the Yanbian Prefecture and taking a six-hour drive along the North Korean border to see the situation firsthand. While there, he'd met with educators, clergy members, State Department personnel, local mayors, prefecture and provincial officials, human rights and refugee advocates, and even China's vice premier.

"The journey to this part of China near the North Korean border," Senator Brownback had written in his report, "has only reinforced my belief that the international community must not neglect the enormous human tragedies of our times: the starvation, depravation, persecution, and direct murder of thousands, and maybe even millions, of the citizens of North Korea. They deserve our intense focus and action."

Back in Washington, Senator Brownback had helped author a bill against sex trafficking in China and elsewhere around the world. He had also sponsored the North Korean Human Rights Act of 2004, which was passed unanimously by both houses of Congress and was signed into law by President George W. Bush in October of that year. This act established the office of Special Envoy for Human Rights in North Korea and authorized $3 million earmarked for defending the refugees and other victims of the North Korean regime.

Senator Brownback had also hosted a Capitol Hill gathering of North Korean refugees who had escaped to the south, and arranged for them to set up a display in the Russell Senate building for senators and the public to learn about their struggles. He had delivered numerous talks on the issue across the country and had been given a hero's welcome on his visit to Los Angeles's Little Korea neighborhood.

Addressing a Los Angeles seminar sponsored by the Korean Congress for North Korean Human Rights and attended by more than one hundred pastors, community leaders, and human rights advocates, Senator Brownback had stated, "I don't know of a worse human rights situation in the world today." He had compared the prison conditions in North Korea to "the horrors of the Soviet Union under Stalin" and the persecuted North Koreans to German Jews during the Holocaust. "You cannot let it take place again on your watch," he had told the assembly. He had urged the Korean-American community to help raise the discussion to "the level of a national debate" and led the congressional effort that eventually opened U.S. borders to North Korean refugees.

Steven's cause was also aided by congressman Royce and Frank Wolf, of Virginia's 10th District; Oklahoma Senator Tom Coburn; and others. Yet none of the public or government outcry seemed to have any effect on the Chinese government's treatment of Steven's case. On the other hand, there was little the Chinese authorities could do to lengthen his term, either. The work credits he had earned were accepted by the officials, and they reduced his sentence accordingly.

The Chinese judicial branch did take one last swipe at Steven: the Beijing court classified him as a "dangerous criminal" and, as was permitted by law, cut his deduction from one year to ten months.

Now Steven had to work hard. In order to be released on schedule, he would have to earn back the two months, but he had little time in which to do it. He would have to almost triple his previous output to make his quota. When he told his fellow church members about his problem, they decided to pitch in and contribute some of the points they'd earned to his account.

"You've done so much for us," said David, one of his fellow inmates, from Cameroon. "Now let us do something for you."

"And it will help us, too," added the Ghanian, Condi. "If you get out early, you can let people know what's happening to North Koreans in China. Maybe then we'll be able to get out, too."

Every day for the next month, three or four inmates dedicated a portion of their work time to Steven's credit. Sometimes, it was only ten or fifteen minutes, sometimes half an hour, but, little by little, they began to whittle away at his extra two months.

The guards were astounded. In none of their experiences had they ever seen this happen. Working together, Steven and his helpers earned the required points in less than a month.

I'm actually going to be released! Steven marveled.

The prison authorities did whatever they could to make Steven's final days in prison as difficult as possible. They denied him outside phone calls, claiming that the lines were down, and withheld his mail. But there was nothing more they could do to delay his release.

19

GOING AND COMING

September 2007

"The LORD is near to all who call on him,
to all who call on him in truth. He fulfills the desires of those who fear
him; he hears their cry and saves them."
—Psalm 145:18–19

As the day for Steven's release approached, he and his fellow prison church members discussed finding a replacement for him. He had led both the Korean- and English-speaking congregations, and now, someone else would have to take charge. "You'll need a new worship leader," he told them. "Otherwise, you might fall into your old ways."

One of the inmates, Stephen from Singapore, seemed a likely choice. He had been a Christian all his life, and his wife was active in the Methodist church. When Steven approached him, however, Stephen declined the offer of leadership. "I don't know how to do it," he said. "I don't think it should be me."

Steven asked him a second time, and then a third, but the man only grew angry. "If you keep pushing me," he told Steven, "I'll stop coming to worship altogether."

In the meantime, neither Helen nor the American consul knew when exactly Steven would be released. When they contacted the prison authorities through the U.S. consulate in Beijing, they were told, "Sometime later—maybe September, maybe as late as November." But Steven felt sure that he would get out soon.

On September 12, the Beijing court official reduced Steven's sentence from five years to four. Even then, the prison officials wouldn't sign the papers or announce his date of release. Steven prayed and tried to practice patience.

One of Steven's cell mates, Lee Jae-Hoon, had been a famous television journalist in South Korea. He'd been arrested for the same offence as Oki—smuggling national treasures, in his case, fossils. Even though he had completed all of the formal government applications and filled out the proper documentation for his purchases, he, too, had been arrested at customs. His sentence was twelve years.

"The press is going to want to talk to you," Jae-Hoon told Steven. "We should work on your interviewing skills." Together, the two went over what Steven would say when he returned to the States—how to look at the cameras, answer questions on his own terms, and generally make a positive impression on the viewing public. Jae-Hoon ran him through a mock interview, throwing questions at him from different angles and correcting him as he responded. He also gave Steven a list of thirty or so questions for which he could have answers prepared.

With only a week remaining before Steven's scheduled release, the prayer group still hadn't decided on a successor. "Okay," Steven addressed them after the Sunday service, "who wants to volunteer? Please, step up. Or, if you have a suggestion, nominate someone else."

After a prolonged discussion, the group realized that no one person would be able to replace Steven. Over the years, he had almost single-handedly revived and then led Christian worship in whichever Chinese prison he was being held. The authorities had tried threatening him, isolating him from the others, and transferring him to another prison. But none of their efforts to stop him had worked.

Instead of naming one person to lead them, the group decided to appoint a committee of four prisoners to coordinate their worship. Two, Donald and Audex, were volunteers; two others, Stephen and Brown, were nominees; but the rest of the group agreed that they were all qualified and that the group would do better with collective leadership.

It's God's will, Steven thought when the group had reached its decision. *No one of them would have been able to do it. They aren't strong enough, and they're more vulnerable. They don't have the protection I enjoyed just from being a U.S. citizen.*

If the prisoners had selected only one leader, he realized, the authorities would have had an easier time breaking down their church—all they would have needed to do would have been to put sufficient pressure on whoever was in charge. With four leaders, however, the authorities wouldn't know who was at the helm. And, even if they managed to take one down, there would still be three others left standing, ready to take his place.

On September 22, a guard came to Steven's door and informed him that he would be released in a few days. The guard then asked him for all his belongings, which Steven promptly collected and turned over. They would be searched, he knew, to make sure he wasn't smuggling anything out—someone else's letters of complaint, for example.

"Where's your passport?" the guard demanded. Before his arrest, Steven had kept his passport with all of his other documents, in his office, but it had been confiscated along with everything else. When he had been in Tiebe, just before his transfer to Yancheng, the authorities had mentioned it, and he'd thought then that maybe there was a chance he'd be released. But it had turned out that they just wanted to send it with him to Beijing.

The prison authorities had called the consulate to inform them of Steven's imminent release. The consul called Helen, and Steven was allowed to phone her. "Send me over a new shirt, trousers, and a pair of shoes and socks," he requested. "And buy me a plane ticket."

"But the consulate said they weren't sure you're coming," she replied. "Are you sure it's really true?"

"Yes," he assured her. "Buy the ticket. If I'm not released, you can change the date. But I want to make sure that there's a ticket waiting to bring me right back to the States—and to *you*."

Everyone was waiting.

The next day, September 23—a Sunday—Steven was summoned to see a prison officer. "There are some questions I need you to answer," the officer told him. "First, by what authority did you hold your daily church meetings in prison? Such meetings are against the law. How were you able to hold them?"

Steven didn't want to tell the man about how the guards had started looking the other way. He wasn't worried about getting them into trouble, but he also didn't want to say anything that could make it more difficult for those prisoners still in Yancheng. "We were very careful," he answered, "and we always made sure to stop if someone was nearby."

"Next," the officer continued, "what power did you exert to bring the prisoners together? How were you able to attract so many? Did you threaten them? Their relatives? Did you pay them money or give them food? How did you get them to disobey the prison rules and join you?"

The Chinese prison system, Steven understood, was run by the strength of power and intimidation. Payments of money or food, and threats of violence to the men or their families, were two of the only motivations they understood—hence the assumption that Steven must have used some manner of physical threat or material reward. Otherwise, they thought, the other men never would have joined him or respected his authority.

"Do you believe in God's power?" Steven asked the officer. "If you can understand the power of the Lord, I can tell you about my authority. That is where it comes from."

The following day, Monday, September 24, Steven faced another set of questions, but this time of a friendlier sort. Whenever a prisoner was about to be released, his fellow inmates would pepper him with queries. "What are your plans?" they'd ask. "What are the first things you're going to do when you get out? What are you going to eat? Where are you going to go?"

The prisoner about to be released almost always had a long, detailed response. Most men's plans involved food, liquor, and women, though not always in that order. A few still had families they wanted to rejoin. Almost everyone would seek out the wide assortment of worldly pleasures he had been denied during his years in prison. Those who were about to be released often spent days and nights planning exactly what they were going to eat and drink, where they would go, and whom they would see.

Steven's fellow inmates were a bit disappointed, therefore, when he had little to tell them. "I don't know," he said. "I don't really have any plans. I used to have so many, but God has cleansed me of my personal desires. I'm surrendered to His will; whatever He wants of me, I will do; wherever He sends me, I will go. Beyond that, I have no idea."

Before his arrest, Steven reflected, he'd had so many ambitions. Now, after four years in prison, he had none. Yet, somehow, he didn't feel any poorer for that. On the contrary, he felt a sense of satisfaction in knowing that this part of his journey was coming to an end and another was about to begin.

Steven laughed to himself as he remembered his expectation, in his first days of prison, that he would be released when he had finished reading the Bible through—and his cell mate Kim Kyong-il's estimate that he'd have to read it not once but ten times. Neither prediction had even come close; the correct number was twenty-one. It had been his sustenance, Steven realized with a sense of thankfulness—his spiritual nourishment and means of survival.

"What will You want of me, Lord?" he prayed that night. "Whatever it is, I'm Yours."

***

"The LORD is good, a refuge in times of trouble. He cares for those who trust in him....This is what the LORD says:...'Now I will break their yoke from your neck and tear your shackles away.'"
—Nahum 1:7, 12–13

Just before noon on Tuesday, two armed guards came to Steven's cell. They escorted him through half an hour's worth of exit procedures and stamped forms, observed him as he changed out of his prison uniform and into the set of clothes Helen had sent, brought him out through the prison's two gates, and ushered him into a waiting white van. They had searched him and his small bag and confiscated a few pictures—a mug shot and some photos cut from magazines.

On September 25, 2007—one day short of the fourth anniversary of his arrest in Chang'an—Steven Kim was released from prison.

A police car with flashing red lights led the van to the Beijing airport, where two policemen walked Steven directly to the Asiana Airlines gate and watched him board the plane for his three-hour flight to Seoul, South Korea.

Steven's twenty-six-year-old son, Charles, who had been working in Guangzhou but hadn't been allowed to join his father in China, was there to meet him at the airport. Steven hugged him and wouldn't let go.

During the two-hour layover before his flight to the U.S., Steven listened as Charles filled him in on everything that had been happening with their family in America and with business in China. Steven couldn't stop smiling as his son shared the news. Eric was doing okay, Charles said; he was back with Helen on Long Island. Lisa had grown up a lot; she wasn't such a girl anymore. Neither of them could wait to see him. Helen had bought a new car. More important, she had opened two new retail stores—and a beautiful showroom that was attracting a lot of attention. The Chang'an office was still in operation. Helen hadn't wanted to bother Steven with all of the details while he was in prison, but he was not surprised to find that she'd kept the business moving forward.

Helen's father had died the year before, Charles told him, in the summer. She had contracted someone to construct a tomb in a cemetery not far from their house. A dozen pastors and scores of other people had attended the funeral. The family had surprised everyone by deciding not to accept condolence money, and several of their Christian Korean friends had consequently chosen to discontinue the practice. Some of the old traditions were dying out, Charles said. Things were changing.

The flight to New York took thirteen hours; Charles, exhausted, slept most of the way. Steven dozed off every now and then, but he was too excited to sleep for very long. Helen had left a message that there would be reporters meeting him at the airport in New York, so he practiced some of the answers he had prepared in prison with Jae-Hoon, rehearsing his delivery.

Steven was especially excited to see Helen. And he hadn't forgotten the promises he'd made in Father School. One of the first things he would do when he got to New York would be to take her out on a date and tell her how much he loved her.

Most of the flight, however, Steven just sat and stared out the window, marveling at the crisp blue sky above them and the billowing gray and white clouds below.

Everything seemed special, magical. He gushed over the airline food, exclaiming that it was delicious. He crunched into a green salad with Italian

Steven is welcomed home at New York's Kennedy Airport.

dressing. How he'd missed fresh greens! And he savored the sweet herbal flavor of the hot Korean tea.

As the plane descended, shortly after dusk, Steven gazed at the New York skyline like a young boy on his first flight. His eyes opened wide, and a smile spread across his face. Lights twinkled from the Manhattan skyscrapers. Everything looked new and different.

"Oh my!" Steven exclaimed to himself. "I'm actually here. I can hardly believe it."

As Steven was deplaning, an airport security guard waiting at the gate called out his name and then offered Steven his hand. "Welcome, Mr. Kim," he said. "It was an honor to serve you. Welcome to the United States. It's good to have you back."

"Thank you," Steven replied, beaming. "It's good to be home."

EPILOGUE

New York

"When his time of service was completed, he returned home."
—Luke 1:23

Though almost sixty years old, Steven Kim felt like an excited teenager again as he stepped onto the tarmac at New York's Kennedy Airport. He could still remember his sensations almost thirty-three years before, when, on first arriving in the city, he had gazed around him in awe at the New York airport. Once again, his heart was practically bursting with happiness and excitement, his head swimming with all that was happening around him. This time, however, he was not venturing into a new land; he was returning home—an adventure of a different sort. Steven had dreamed of this moment for four full years, ever since he had heard the first prison door slam shut behind him. Now, his dream had become a reality.

More than ever before, the U.S. was to Steven a nation of salvation, a champion-state of equality, individualism, and democracy—of personal, economic, and religious freedom. He'd taken those things for granted, he now realized, but he would never make that mistake again. Nor would he take for granted the grace of God. Steven remembered Psalm 119:71: *"It was good for me to be afflicted so that I might learn your decrees."*

Steven looked around him and up at the sky above. "Dear God," he prayed aloud, "thank You." Then, he crossed toward the terminal, with no idea of the future that awaited him around even the first corner.

When Steven had passed through customs and entered the terminal, he was greeted by a cheering crowd of family, friends, and well-wishers. Brightly decorated banners celebrated his return, printed with phrases such as "Welcome Home, Steven!" and "Steven Kim, American Hero!" Balloons flew overhead, and a group of relatives held out bunches of flowers. People were clapping and shouting Steven's name. Cameras flashed as reporters called for him to turn their way.

"You look so well," Helen exclaimed, "so peaceful and calm!"

Steven gave a brief statement to the press, thanking everyone for the support and for welcoming him on his return. When a reporter from *Korea Central Daily News* asked him, "Mr. Kim, are you going to continue your rescue work for North Korean refugees?" Steven answered without hesitation, "In the past, I helped North Korean refugees who came to me for help. From now on, I will go out to them to help."

An entourage of vehicles caravanned back to the Kims' house on Long Island, where Steven gathered with his family and a few good friends for a prayer service. It felt so good to be there, Steven told them. He didn't think he could have survived without knowing that they were all supporting him back home.

Much to Steven's relief, the next few weeks were pretty quiet; people seemed to be willing to give him time alone with his family. As soon as he and Helen had the chance, they stole away together for dinner at her favorite restaurant in the city. But, before long, the phone started to ring, and once it did, it seemed that it would never stop.

Steven's release had been given broad coverage by both human rights organizations and the mainstream American press, with ABC News reporting, "After years of requests from the State Department and U.S. lawmakers, China has released an American humanitarian volunteer it had held for four years on trafficking charges."

Steven's hometown of Huntington, New York, honored him with a proclamation from the town board. "One of the greatest rights our forefathers bestowed upon us in America is the right to worship as we choose," said Councilman Mark Cuthbertson. "I am proud to recognize the extraordinary efforts of one man who fought for the rights of others less fortunate than himself."

Steven and Helen at a ceremony in their honor

"In most civilized countries," Suzanne Scholte reminded the public, "a person of Kim's compassion and concern for his fellow man would have been lauded and praised and admired. This American businessman who traveled frequently to China saw people suffering and in great need, and, because he was a Christian, he could not turn his back on them. Thus, working with the support of his home church, New York Presbyterian Church, in Long Island City, he raised funds to provide food and shelter to North Korean refugees until they were healthy enough to travel to South Korea, and then, he helped them make their way to freedom....To my knowledge, there is no humanitarian worker—American, South Korean, or Japanese—who has been arrested for this crime and served a longer sentence than Steven Kim."

Soon after his release from prison in 2007, Steven Kim protests across from the Chinese Embassy in Washington, D.C.

Notices of Steven's release helped raise increased awareness of the plight of North Korean refugees and, indeed, all North Koreans. "I am optimistic that this recognition will highlight the struggles of North Korean refugees," Councilman Cuthbertson stated at the Huntington ceremony honoring Steven, "and I encourage more citizens to become involved."

***

"Defend the cause of the weak and fatherless; maintain the rights of the poor and oppressed. Rescue the weak and needy; deliver them from the hand of the wicked."
—Psalm 82:3–4

Since his release, Steven has addressed numerous political, religious, human rights, school, and civic groups about his experiences and the plight of North Korean refugees. "[He] has," in the words of a respondent to the ABC piece, "become a face and a voice on behalf of suffering North Koreans." The

Steven and Suzanne Scholte at a rally for North Korean refugees outside Union Station in Washington, D.C.

situation for refugees in China, Steven quickly discovered upon his return to the States, had not improved during his time in prison. If anything, conditions had deteriorated. Today, the vast majority of those crossing the border from North Korea into China are women, and the human traffickers are more active than ever.

In Washington, D.C., at a rally outside Union Station protesting the violent treatment, imprisonment, and repatriation of North Korean refugees, Steven announced his new mission: to rescue trafficked North Korean women and children. As founder and executive director of 318 Partners for North Korean Refugees, he has redoubled his efforts to help children who have been victimized and women who have been sold into forced marriages and the sex trade. Using the underground railroad that he established in China, as well as new routes going through Laos, the group has successfully rescued half a dozen such women, but Steven is painfully aware that this is hardly a drop in the bucket from an ocean of suffering.

In addition to his work with refugees in China, Steven's efforts have shifted into North Korea itself. During a visit there, Steven discovered that there were already 176 underground churches in North Korea. Steven said, "Now I understood that this was my mission. God was building a highway to freedom." Partnering with Youth With a Mission (YWAM), Steven is building an underground "gospel railroad," by which refugees can move from one haven to another.

The urgent requests for assistance Steven receives regularly from North Korean refugees remind him of how much work remains to be done. Looking for donors to help sponsor women and children in need, he sends out requests in a monthly mission newsletter.

One letter narrates a young boy's life as a "flower swallow," the name given to the North Korean children who live on the city streets and town squares of China and North Korea, begging, scavenging, stealing, and selling themselves for food.

My father passed away because of malnutrition, so my mother took care of us, but then she went to China, leaving us in North Korea. My brother and I became flower swallow kids who lived by begging and picking up food from the ground, wandering around the market places or train station. I became a flower swallow kid when I was thirteen. I saw two or three people die at the station every day. The security police were the worst to us. They oppressed us with beatings and sometimes raped the girls. We were often beaten so hard, we couldn't walk.

One day, a security officer poured boiling water on my legs. They were burned so severely that I couldn't walk for about three months. I had to crawl to beg to survive. Then, I crossed to China…I got a job at Harbin City. However, even though I worked hard for a month or two, most of them didn't pay me. Rather, they threatened me to tell the police about me if I kept demanding pay…. I am always on the run from the Chinese police officers.

Please help me go to South Korea, or any other place where I can get citizenship and learn about God more deeply. I believe you. I think you are an angel God sent me. When I am in deep despair, I think of you and the ones who pray for me to get refreshed.

Another plea came from a young girl who crossed the Tumen River with her mother in 2006. As soon as they got to the other side, she said, they were met by a man who told them he could find them work and a place to stay. When they went with him, however, he abused them and then sold them to a man in Yanji. There were three other North Korean women already at the man's apartment when they arrived, "doing adult sex chatting by showing all parts of their bodies through a camera in the computer. Usually they used young girls for this work." The young girl's account continued:

Then, he told me to take off my clothes and do as I was instructed by the man in the computer. If I didn't do that, he threatened, he would sell me to a disabled man. He said it would be better to show my body by just doing sexual chatting over the video than to be sexually harassed by disabled partners. I thought I had no choice at this time. So I told him I would work.

Then, later, the Korean-Chinese boss called me out to sleep with him. I refused. Then, he beat me and raped me that night. How cruel he was. He was like an animal.

The next morning, he asked me if I wanted to do the sex chatting, so I said no. Then, he started beating me in front of my mother. My mother was trying to stop him and apologized to him and said she would persuade me to do the job. So I had to do that dirty job.

But not long after, my mother and I had to part because she was sold to a mentally disabled man in the countryside of Shandong Province because she was too old for that job. After my mother left me, I couldn't eat and wanted to kill myself, so I ate any kind of pills I could find. I was really miserable.

Since I was locked in the chatting place, it wasn't easy to escape. So I had to pretend to be good to the boss by doing whatever he wanted me to do. My request to him was to sell me to a place near where my mother was sold. Every day, I asked him to sell me because I missed my mother so much. Then, the boss sold me for 3,000 yuan. Right now there are still fifteen North Korean women who are working as slaves at the sex chatting place in Yanji.

To be with my mother, I became another man's sexual partner, as he wanted. I was also sold to a disabled man. Every night, when he approached me with a strange smile, I tried to resist, but I couldn't stop him. I always cried, thinking of my mother, who was nearby.

The parents of this disabled man had locked the door from the outside so I couldn't escape. I had to live at that house like a prisoner. Finally, I freed myself from them, and my mother did the same. I am now living at a hiding place with my mother. It is not easy for us to live like this all the time. We want to go to Korea. Please help us out of this place soon.

Another letter came from a girl who had first crossed the border in 1999.

I had lost my father when I was 2 years old. It was like a war zone... dead bodies here and there. At that time, there was a group of people who came from China to help North Korean people by offering jobs. They looked so kind, righteous, and thankful. So I followed them into China. I was pregnant at the time.

But they sold me to other people for 3,000 yuan and disappeared. From that time, my desperate and long runaway life began.

She escaped from her first owner, still pregnant, and climbed twenty miles over a mountain, only to be captured again in Yanji and sold to a county in Liaoning Province, where there were no other Koreans.

They locked me in a room and sexually abused, harassed, and raped me numerous times before I escaped from them.... Then, the day was approaching to deliver my baby. My belly was getting bigger. But I couldn't have my baby delivered by my own ability. I allowed myself to be sold for the third time to a man in a nearby Tianjin City by a trafficker.... From the first day, the owner of the apartment locked me in and, a few days later, he came and talked [with another man] in a language I couldn't understand. Then, they forced me to do a disgusting sex act. When I resisted, they beat me savagely and kicked me in my belly. Then they raped me.

I couldn't resist, because if I did, they would report me to the Chinese police and I would be repatriated to North Korea. I had no choice but to take all the humiliation.

These newsletters are accompanied by an appeal: "If anyone wishes to help this woman, please contact 318 Partners Mission, Rescue Team for the Trafficked Women in China." There is no shortage of tragic stories coming out of China and North Korea, and there is no end to the work still left for Steven Kim and others like him.

***

"The LORD himself goes before you and will be with you; he will never leave you nor forsake you. Do not be afraid; do not be discouraged."
—Deuteronomy 31:8

Speaking to a church group early in 2009, Steven was asked a question regarding what he had learned in prison: What was the one thing he would take away from the experience?

At first, he was unsure how to answer. Then, he remembered Chang Kwang-Jin, the mob boss he had met in Tiebe, and felt overwhelmed by how fortunate he'd been in so many ways.

"When I was in prison," he told the assembly, "I met a killer—a gang leader whose victims' blood had barely dried on his hands. He hadn't yet found God, hadn't yet let Him into his life. He'd thought he was the ruler of the universe. But even this murderer became like a child and begged for forgiveness when he was met with human compassion and with the fathomless mercy of the Lord. I recited to him this psalm:

> *I call with all my heart; answer me, O Lord, and I will obey your decrees. I call out to you; save me and I will keep your statutes. I rise before dawn and cry for help; I have put my hope in your word. My eyes stay open through the watches of the night, that I may meditate on your promises. Hear my voice in accordance with your love; preserve my life, O Lord, according to your laws. Those who devise wicked schemes are near, but they are far from your law. Yet you are near, O Lord, and all your commands are true.* (Psalm 119:145–151)

"No matter how alone we might feel in this world, I learned—how hopeless our life may seem—God is always near us; He is always by our side."

Steven prays over China during one of his missionary trips.

ABOUT THE AUTHORS

Carl Herzig, PhD, is a fellow of the National Writing Project and a reviewer for several literary and creative arts journals. He leads student service-learning trips to India and has served as an Iowa Humanities Scholar and evaluator for the Hearst Foundation U.S. Senate Youth Program, the Iowa Humanities Board, and the Illinois Council for the Humanities. He is currently professor of English at St. Ambrose University in Davenport, Iowa, where he teaches courses in sacred poetry, contemporary fiction, and creative and expository writing.

***

Today, Steven Kim's home in Huntington, New York, is a stark contrast to the prison cells he shared with dozens of felons. He now runs 318 Partners (www.318partners.org), a U.S.-based nonprofit organization dedicated to rescuing North Korean women and orphans from forced labor and sex trafficking in China. He is also partnering with YWAM (Youth With a Mission) to plant underground churches in North Korea.